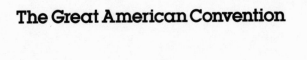

The Great American Convention

The Great American Convention

A Political History of Presidential Elections

Gary C. Byrne and Paul Marx

PACIFIC BOOKS, PUBLISHERS
Palo Alto, California

International Standard Book Number 0-87015-220-3.
Library of Congress Catalog Card Number 76-14102.
Printed and bound in the United States of America.

PACIFIC BOOKS, PUBLISHERS
P. O. Box 558, Palo Alto, California 94302

For Norma, Silas, and Tristan

Contents

The Great American Convention

The Great American Crime Jar?

CHAPTER ONE

Introduction

The president of the United States is probably the most powerful man in the world. This book presents a narrow view of the
way he is selected. A man becomes president through a two-step
process. First, he is selected by a major party to be the leader of
that party's national ticket, and second, he is selected by the nation's electorate through another two-step process to head the
nation's executive branch of government.

This book will attempt to explain how the first selection process, the national party nominating conventions, affects the second selection process, the nationwide general elections held on
the first Tuesday after the first Monday in November every four
years.

The material attempting to explain why the conventions nominate the men they do and why the conventions function the way
they do is voluminous. Some of the most interesting and infor-
mative works on conventions are listed in the bibliography.

The basic argument of this book is that the first step in the
process of selecting a president, the nominating conventions,
reflect the moods and strengths of the competing parties and
also act to determine how cohesive and forceful the parties will
be in carrying their presidential campaigns to the people. This
idea was first popularized by Paul David, Ralph Goldman, and
Richard Bain in *The Politics of National Party Conventions.*
Whereas they gave the theory only brief consideration, we have
attempted to systematize the theoretical relationship between
conventions and presidential elections and use it as a predicting
device.

We have developed a convention formula that divides the fifty-four nominating conventions between 1864 and 1968 into six basic styles. Each of these styles is indicative of the strength of the parties as they proceed into the November election and of the amount of appeal each ticket will have to the general electorate.

The most powerful type of presidential nominating convention is the kind we call a conciliatory convention or Type A. This type of convention produced no candidates between 1864 and 1968 who received fewer popular votes than their opponents. In one instance, though, a Type A convention produced a presidential candidate who lost the election to his opponent by one electoral vote even though he received several hundred thousand more votes than did the victor. In the 1876 election Rutherford B. Hayes defeated Samuel Tilden although Tilden won a popular plurality. Tilden was the candidate of a conciliatory convention, while Hayes was the candidate of a much less powerful type of convention.

Next in strength to the conciliatory convention is the convention of continuity or the Type B convention. The Type B convention has produced only one candidate who received fewer popular votes than his opponent, Herbert Hoover, who lost to Franklin Roosevelt in 1932. Roosevelt happened to be a Type A candidate. The 1932 election was the first since 1864 in which a Type B candidate and a Type A candidate came face to face. One Type B candidate, Grover Cleveland, actually received more votes than his opponent, Benjamin Harrison, in 1888 but lost the presidency when Harrison gained more electoral votes.

Type B candidates usually receive more popular votes than their opponents except when they run against Type A candidates.

Type C conventions, or steamroller conventions, have historically produced candidates who win against every opponent except those nominated by Type A and B conventions.

The next strongest convention is known as a Type D or compromise convention. Type D conventions have always produced candidates who defeat the nominees of either Type E or F conventions but who always receive fewer popular votes than Type

A, B, or C candidates. In two cases, Hayes versus Tilden in 1876 and Harrison versus Cleveland in 1888, the Type D nominee defeated the candidate of a more powerful convention, but in both cases the Type D nominees received fewer popular votes than did their opponents.

Type E conventions, or conventions of incumbent conflict, have always produced losing candidates. Since 1864 no candidate nominated by a Type E convention has ever won the general election.

The weakest type of political convention, historically, has been the Type F or incumbent failure convention. The only convention of this type since 1864 was held in 1884, when the Republican party refused to renominate Chester A. Arthur and, instead, selected James G. Blaine. Blaine went on to lose to Grover Cleveland in the November election.

Our formula, then, divides all major party conventions between 1864 and 1968 into six types running from A to F. These types are then rank-ordered. From this rank ordering, conventions are classified as strong or weak. We find that the strongest conventions produce Type A candidates, who always receive more popular votes than their opponents. The next strongest convention produces Type B candidates, who always receive more popular votes than their opponents except when they run against Type A nominees. Type C candidates get more popular votes than D, E, or F nominees but fewer popular votes than either Type A or B. Type D candidates always get fewer popular votes than Types A, B, or C but more than either Type E or F. Types E and F have always received fewer popular votes than their opponents and have never won a presidential election.

Thus it can be seen that the mode of nomination can be a critical factor in determining the outcome of presidential races. This fact does not suggest, however, that conventions cause electoral success. Rather, it means that the conventions are indicators of the probability that a party will be strong enough or cohesive enough or vigorous enough to defeat the opposition.

In Chapter Three each of these convention types will be discussed and the relationship between convention style and general election outcome will be examined.

TABLE 1: *Votes Received by Presidential Candidates, 1864-1968*

YEAR	CANDIDATE	REPUBLICAN TYPE	NO. OF VOTES	VS. CANDIDATE	DEMOCRAT TYPE	NO. OF VOTES
1864	Lincoln	B	2,216,067	McClellan	C	1,808,725
1868	Grant	C	3,015,071	Seymour	D	2,709,615
1872	Grant	B	3,597,070	Greeley	C	2,834,079
1876	Hayes	D	4,033,950	Tilden	A	4,284,757
1880	Garfield	D	4,449,053	Hancock	D	4,442,030
1884	Blaine	F	4,848,334	Cleveland	D	4,911,017
1888	Harrison	D	5,444,337	Cleveland	B	5,540,050
1892	Harrison	E	5,190,902	Cleveland	C	5,554,414
1896	McKinley	C	7,035,638	Bryan	D	6,467,940
1900	McKinley	B	7,219,530	Bryan	C	6,358,017
1904	Roosevelt	B	7,628,834	Parker	C	5,084,491
1908	Taft	C	7,679,006	Bryan	C	6,409,106
1912	Taft	E	3,483,922	Wilson	D	6,286,214
1916	Hughes	D	8,538,221	Wilson	B	9,129,606
1920	Harding	D	16,152,200	Cox	D	9,147,253
1924	Coolidge	B	15,725,016	Davis	D	8,385,586
1928	Hoover	C	21,392,190	Smith	C	15,761,841
1932	Hoover	B	15,761,841	Roosevelt	A	22,821,857
1936	Landon	C	16,679,853	Roosevelt	B	27,751,957
1940	Willkie	D	22,304,755	Roosevelt	B	27,243,466
1944	Dewey	C	22,006,278	Roosevelt	B	25,602,505
1948	Dewey	D	21,970,065	Truman	B	24,105,812
1952	Eisenhower	A	33,936,252	Stevenson	D	27,314,992
1956	Eisenhower	B	35,585,316	Stevenson	C	26,031,322
1960	Nixon	C	34,108,596	Kennedy	A	34,227,096
1964	Goldwater	C	27,176,799	Johnson	B	43,126,506
1968	Nixon	A	31,783,783	Humphrey	C	31,271,839

In Chapters Four through Fourteen we will analyze eleven different elections between 1864 and 1968. In each of these discussions we will contrast competing nomination styles and show how the nominating style affected the chances for victory of the major candidates.

CHAPTER TWO

The Emergence of Presidential Nominating Conventions

Nothing in the Constitution of the United States establishes or recommends national party conventions as we know them to-day.[1] In the years between the ratification of the Constitution and the first national nominating convention, two very different types of systems were used to select American presidents.

The first system was the one contemplated by the framers of the Constitution. This method, which was used to elect George Washington, attempted to combine the nominating process and the electoral process. The Constitution states in regard to the election of the president that, "Each State shall appoint . . . a number of electors, equal to the whole number of Senators and Representatives to which the State may be entitled in the Congress: . . . The electors shall . . . vote by Ballot for two Persons,

---

[1]For further study into the history of the presidential nominating conventions, the following works provide points of departure: Richard C. Bain, *Convention Decisions and Voting Records* (Washington: Brookings Institution, 1960); Paul T. David, Ralph M. Goldman, and Richard C. Bain, *The Politics of National Party Conventions* (New York: Vintage Books, 1964); Herbert Eaton, *Presidential Timber: A History of Nominating Conventions, 1898–1960* (New York: Free Press of Glencoe, 1964); S. E. Morrison, "The First National Nominating Convention," *American Historical Review,* 17 (1912), 744–63; M. Ostrogorskii, "The Rise and Fall of the Nominating Caucus, Legislative and Congressional," *American Historical Review,* 5 (1900), 255–59; Gerald Pomper, *Nominating the President* (Evanston, Ill.: Northwestern University Press, 1963); Eugene H. Roseboom, *A History of Presidential Elections* (New York: Macmillan, 1959); Arthur M. Schlesinger, Jr. (ed.), *History of American Presidential Elections, 1789–1968* (New York: Chelsea House, 1971); and Charles S. Thompson, *The Rise and Fall of the Congressional Caucus* (New Haven, Conn.: Yale University, 1902).

of whom one at least shall not be an inhabitant of the Same state with themselves" (Art. II, Sec. 1).

In other words, the state legislatures could select presidential electors in any manner they chose. These electors, who were equal in number to the states' members in both houses of Congress, would then meet and vote for two candidates. The person receiving the highest number of votes from the electors of the various states would then be declared president-elect, and the person receiving the second highest total would be vice president-elect. There was no anticipated elimination process and the number of potential candidates could be quite large.

This method of selecting the president of the United States was based on the notion that a natural aristocracy of men existed whose virtue and wisdom made them natural candidates for the presidency. According to this notion, selecting a president was simply a matter of searching through this natural aristocracy and selecting the individual who possessed the greatest virtue and the greatest wisdom. The problem, of course, was to devise some method for sorting out the best person from this natural aristocracy.

Many of the Virginia delegates to the Constitutional Convention proposed that Congress choose the president. This method of selecting the president, however, violated the principle of separation of powers, and the framers of the Constitution could not accept the principle of separation of powers and at the same time establish a procedure for selecting the chief executive which depended upon his acceptance by the Congress.

One Massachusetts delegate suggested that the president be selected by the governors of the various states. This procedure was unacceptable to the founders because it would have weakened the authority of the federal government over the states. It would, in fact, have given the states tremendous power over the federal government, because, in the long run, the chief executive of the federal government would probably have become little more than a tool of the more powerful state leaders.

Another method suggested was direct election of the president by the people. This was not acceptable to the framers of the

Constitution for several reasons, but primarily because it was believed that the electorate, even though it was strictly limited at this time, possessed neither the information nor the moral standards needed to judge which of the natural aristocracy was most fit to be president.

The members of the Constitutional Convention eventually decided to select the president at a temporary meeting of delegates called electors from each of the states. These electors would comprise what was to be called the "electoral college." The electors, who were to be the most capable individuals from each of the states, would, in their great wisdom, decide who in the thirteen states was the wisest and most virtuous member of the natural aristocracy, and thus who should serve as president. The person judged second best by the electors would be designated vice-president. Each state was allowed to choose its electoral slate by whatever means it deemed best.

The first sixty-nine presidential electors met in February 1789 to choose the president. In 1789 the decision was not a difficult one. George Washington was considered a military genius, he had led a successful revolution, and he had presided over the Constitutional Convention. One of the leading citizens of Virginia, Washington was also one of the richest men in the country.

The second election for president in 1792 remained a relatively simple matter, with each of the 132 electors—increased over the first election by virtue of several new states—pledging their votes to George Washington, but the vice-presidency was hotly contested. During the years between 1789 and 1792, it became apparent to a number of political leaders that the selection of the president and vice-president was a critical decision, one which held the kernel of tremendous revolutionary potential in the United States. There was no serious question about giving George Washington a second term in office, but the anti-monarchy Republicans chose their own candidate, George Clinton, to oppose the incumbent, Vice-President John Adams. Adams won 77 votes to Clinton's 50. The struggle over the vice-presidency indicated that the battle lines were being drawn.

By 1796 political parties had begun to form, and it was becoming clear that the next contest for the presidency would be both contested and close. It was also apparent that the provision in Article II that each elector vote for two persons without indicating a preference between them could cause serious problems. Both in 1789 and in 1792, when each elector gave one vote to Washington and another vote to someone else, the problem was not severe. But the split in the vote for the vice-presidency in 1792 indicated the growing strength of the two major factions in Congress.

By 1796 it was evident that with 138 electors (the increase in electors followed the growth of the young Congress) it would be possible to have many different candidates, each of whom might receive only a few votes. Furthermore, if enough electors voted for the same vice-presidential candidate, they could give him the presidency if none of the presidential candidates received a sufficient number of first-place votes.

If the actions of electors were to be coordinated in a drive to select a particular individual for the presidency, some sort of leadership structure was necessary. On one side the Federalists were led by Alexander Hamilton. The other side was led by Thomas Jefferson and James Madison. By the summer of 1796, the Jefferson-Madison group had decided that the best way of resolving the problem resulting from the constitutional ambiguity about the selection of the president and vice-president was to hold a congressional caucus to nominate candidates for those two offices. If a group of like-minded men could agree on two candidates, they decided, it might be possible to avoid the problems inherent in Article II of the Constitution. Also, by uniting forces with like-minded political leaders they would improve their chances of having their candidate selected as president.

In 1796, the Jefferson-Madison forces were known as the Republicans. The Republicans in Congress held a caucus that summer and selected Thomas Jefferson as their presidential candidate and Senator Aaron Burr of New York as the vice-presidential nominee.

The 138 electors met in December. The combination of constitutional ambiguity and budding political parties led to considerable confusion. Thirteen candidates received votes. John Adams received 71 votes, an absolute majority, and gained the presidency. Thomas Jefferson became vice-president with 68 votes, and an awkward situation resulted. John Adams, the candidate of the Federalist party, and Thomas Jefferson, the candidate of the Republican party, were placed together as president and vice-president. Thomas Pinckney of South Carolina, Adams' running mate, received 59 votes, and Aaron Burr, Thomas Jefferson's running mate, received only 30 votes. Apparently twelve of the electors who supported Adams voted for someone other than Pinckney.

The outcome of the 1796 election, in which the president and the vice-president were chosen from different parties, reinforced the belief in many minds that something had to be done to more properly structure and guide the presidential selection process.

In 1800 a new problem in the procedures for selecting the president appeared: the possibility of a tie vote between two candidates of the same party. If all of the Republican electors cast their votes for the presidential and vice-presidential candidates of that party, and more Republican electors cast votes than Federalist electors, there would be a tie for the presidency between the two Republican candidates, and the contest would be thrown into the House of Representatives.

The problem of a tie vote arose because no provision had been made to designate which vote of the electors was for the president and which was for the vice-president. The electors simply voted for two men; the candidate with the highest number became president, and the candidate with the second highest became vice-president.

One consequence of failure to designate the office for which the elector was voting had been the election of a president from one party and a vice-president from another party in 1796. Some of the electors did not follow party instructions. They voted for the proper presidential candidate but not for the designated vice-presidential candidate. One elector apparently went so far as to vote for one of the presidential candidates for president and the other presidential candidate for vice-president. Because the votes had equal weight, it was possible to use both presidential and vice-presidential votes to win either office. Thus, the presidential candidate of the Republican party, Thomas Jefferson, was able to acquire enough votes to become vice-president to the Federalist president, Adams.

In 1800 the Republican organization, which was supporting Thomas Jefferson for president and Aaron Burr for vice-president, apparently did a superb job. The outcome of that election highlighted the difficulty and, to an extent, the absurdity of the election process devised by the framers of the Constitution. Thomas Jefferson, the Republican presidential candidate, received 73 votes, but so did the Republican vice-presidential candidate, Aaron Burr. This 73—73 tie for the presidency resulted because no way existed to distinguish between presidential votes and vice-presidential votes. The election of 1800 was then thrown into the House of Representatives and, ironically, it was left up to a lame duck Federalist-controlled Congress to select between the two Republican candidates who had tied for the presidency. It would have been possible for the Federalists to frustrate Jefferson, the party leader, by selecting Burr as president, but Alexander Hamilton convinced the Federalist congressmen that Thomas Jefferson was the more incorruptible of the two and, thus, Jefferson became the nation's third president.

The success of the congressional caucus in providing some structure and control over the selection process designed by the Constitution waned very rapidly, although the procedure itself lasted until 1824. By that time it was becoming obvious that even a president as potentially strong as James Monroe was virtually stripped of his power by the presidential selection process. Monroe owed his nomination to the members of his party in Congress. His fellow party members in Congress, however, did not depend upon him for their own reelection to Congress because at that time there was no effective opposition party.

Without some control over the members of his party in Congress, Monroe was reduced to the point where he could preside

over his country but could not exercise the power commensu-
rate with his position as chief executive.

At the same time the political environment in the country as a
whole was changing rapidly. Suffrage was being extended, and
the influence of states that had formerly held much of the power
in the original thirteen colonies was being reduced. Virginia,
once the most populous state, had dropped to third place.
Urban centers were becoming areas of political power as
increasing numbers of working-class wage-earners were en-
franchised. The western areas were also growing, both in population and in determination to exert a greater impact on
political affairs. Also, by 1824 the Federalist party had disappeared, and the country possessed only one major political
party, the Democratic-Republican party.

Because Monroe was virtually unopposed in 1820, the congressional caucus did not function in its usual form. Opposition
to the congressional caucus was growing stronger, and by 1824
it had become intense. Use of the congressional caucus gave to
the Congress power that belonged to the people. By choosing
the candidate or candidates for the presidency itself, the Congress deprived noncongressional forces of power and influence
and proceeded to create a president wholly dependent upon
congressional support for nomination and election. Congressional selection of the president was hardly the model of checks
and balances the framers had envisioned.

At the same time, support was growing rapidly in most of the
states for a movement toward selecting presidential electors by
popular vote rather than having them appointed by the legislatures as had been traditionally done in most states. By 1824
eighteen of the twenty-four states were selecting their presidential electors by popular vote. In the six other states presidential
electors were still appointed by the state legislature.

In 1824, Andrew Jackson won 99 of the 261 electoral votes
cast for president. The runner-up, John Quincy Adams, won 84
votes. With neither candidate receiving a majority, the election
was thrown into the House of Representatives. When the members of the House selected Adams, Jackson was understand-
ably furious. In 1825 he resigned from the Senate to begin his

campaign for the presidency in 1828. Senator Martin Van Buren of New York, the leader of the anti-Adams forces in Congress, suggested that a national convention be called to nominate candidates for the 1828 election. But no conventions were held, and Andrew Jackson was swept to the presidency with 178 electoral votes.

Jackson owed nothing to either congressional caucuses or to any members of Congress for his election. He came to power as the leader of a highly organized, broadly based popular movement. The election of 1828 saw the development of a new type of party politics: the development of mass political parties which could select a man for the presidency without being dominated by Congress.

With the Jackson victory in 1828, it became apparent that a presidential nominating process would have to be developed which would bring structure to the presidential selection process and at the same time free the president of his former dependency upon Congress. On September 11, 1830, the new Anti-Mason party, which had developed among anti-Jackson groups in western New York and Massachusetts, held the first national party convention.

By 1831, the National Republican party, which was the old John Quincy Adams group in Congress, had dwindled so significantly that some device was needed to give it a semblance of nationwide support. So, on December 12, 1831, the National Republicans met in a national convention and nominated Henry Clay for president.

The Democratic-Republican party, or the Jacksonians, were also having their problems by 1832. The basic split was that between Vice-President John C. Calhoun of South Carolina and Secretary of State Van Buren. The leaders of the party, seeking a means of pulling the party together, decided that a nationwide convention could be used to unite the party and to capitalize on President Jackson's widespread popularity. It was argued that the convention should be held after Congress had adjourned so that members of Congress would be unable to exert undue influence on the convention proceedings.

The Democratic-Republican convention followed the Anti-

convention in three basic procedures: "Each state could
own judgment in choosing delegates; delegate votes were
ed on the electoral college basis; and a special majority,
thirds, was required for nomination."[2] At the Democratic-
Republican convention held on May 21 and May 22, 1832,
Jackson was unanimously renominated. Van Buren was nominated for the vice-presidency, winning 208 votes to 75 for
Calhoun.

At this particular convention only one ballot was needed to
nominate both the president and vice-president, but rules were
established then to provide for nomination when more than one
ballot was required. It was decided that if no selection could be
made on the first ballot, the various state delegations would
caucus and prepare to vote on a second ballot. This balloting,
caucusing, reballoting, and recaucusing would then continue
until one candidate received the two-thirds majority required
for nomination.

The national convention system was initiated as a method of
selecting candidates for the presidency that would give form and
continuity to the ambiguous provisions in the Constitution, and
that would release the president from the tight grip of congressional control. With the political party system in flux in the
1830s, it took several years to establish the authority of the
conventions to determine presidential nominations. Thereafter,
nominating conventions of the major parties were held regularly
during presidential election years. These conventions provided
the legitimizing structure that could allow citizen input and
bring a proper coherence and order to the selection of America's president.

[2] David, Goldman, and Bain, *op. cit.*, p. 55.

CHAPTER THREE

Nominating Conventions
and Presidential Elections

Political parties do not generally win presidential elections by taking votes away from the opposition. Presidential elections are normally won by the party that is most effective in mobilizing its own voters and appealing to the broad mass of independents and new voters. The number of voters who move back and forth between the parties in successive elections has traditionally been relatively small. In their book, *The Ticket-Splitters,* Walter DeVries and Lance Tarrance argue that the number of these ticket-splitters is increasing rapidly. Nevertheless, it remains apparent that the vast majority of voters stay with one or the other of the two major parties.[1]

The most outstanding example in recent times of the movement of a large number of voters from one party to the other in a presidential election occurred in 1932. In the presidential contest between Franklin Roosevelt and Herbert Hoover, the Republican vote declined by 26 percent from 1928 while the Democratic vote increased by 52 percent in the same period.

Between the years 1896 and 1960, the absolute number of people voting for president increased on the average of about 11 percent for each election period. Each party could improve its

---

[1]See especially Angus Campbell, et al., *The American Voter* (New York: John Wiley & Sons, 1960); Angus Campbell, et al., *Elections and the Political Order* (New York: John Wiley & Sons, 1966). For another perspective see V. O. Key, Jr., *The Responsible Electorate: Rationality in Presidential Voting, 1936–1960* (New York: Vintage Books, 1968); Walter DeVries and Lance Tarrance, *The Ticket-Splitters: A New Force in American Politics* (Grand Rapids: William B. Eerdmans Publishing Co., 1972).

level of support by 11 percent for each election, therefore, merely by adding the average number of new voters coming into the electorate, assuming that the turnout rates remained basically stable. If one party is able to capture a larger proportion of this 11 percent average increase than the other party, it stands a good chance of winning the election.[2]

The primary concern of a political party in presidential elections is not to win voters from the opposition party but rather to maximize the proportion of its own partisans who vote and the proportion of the independent vote and the new vote that can be attracted to its ticket. During a presidential campaign the parties normally do not have time to raid each other for support. Each party must use all of its resources to keep its own partisans in line and appeal to the independents and the new voters just entering the electorate. Keeping one's own usual constituency in line and appealing to independents and new voters require a high level of party organization and party morale.

The presidential nominating conventions reflect the organizational capabilities and unifying forces existent within the parties and indicate the cohesiveness and strength the parties will possess as they move from the convention into the presidential campaign. Our formula for predicting the outcomes of presidential campaigns by studying national party conventions is highly dependent upon these forces.

It is important to keep in mind that parties win presidential elections primarily by rallying and mobilizing their own forces and by appealing to independents and new voters rather than by attracting voters who normally adhere to the opposition party. Thus, it is more important to have a candidate around whom the party can unify and mobilize its resources than to have a candidate who may be highly attractive to partisans of the opposition party. The national party conventions are the focal points at which the unifying and mobilizing abilities of the parties are probably best tested and best publicized. The formula

[2]See Paul T. David, Ralph M. Goldman, and Richard C. Bain, *The Politics of National Party Conventions* (New York: Vintage Books, 1964), p. 295.

we have developed attempts to utilize the behavior of delegates to the national party conventions in order to measure the ability of the political parties to rally around a party leader and to generate cohesive and mobilizing forces that can carry a party to victory in the general election.

NATIONAL PARTY CONVENTIONS FROM A TO F

Our formula divides the national party conventions from 1864 through 1968 into six distinct types. The year 1864 is used as a starting date because that is the year during which the two-party system as we know it today began to function. The Republican party ran in its first presidential election in 1856, and the election of 1860 saw four major parties enter the race for the presidency. Thus, the 1864 election was the first in which we had a face-to-face contest between the Republican party and the Democratic party, which was followed by an uninterrupted series of contests between these two parties.

The six types of conventions described by our model are distinguished by the levels of conflict and harmony that dominate them. The formula is built on the assumption that the levels of conflict and harmony that attend nominating conventions are indicative of the strengths of the political parties as they wage their contest for the presidency. The formula does not argue that conflict is always bad and harmony is always good, but rather contends that the level that characterizes a given convention is conducive to victory or defeat, depending upon the current political environment. As a general rule, we have found that conflict accompanying the nomination of the in-party candidate is a negative sign. But it is usually a favorable sign when harmony accompanies the in-party nominating process. When conflict characterizes the out-party nominating convention, the probability that the out-party will win the election is usually increased. An out-party nominating process characterized by harmony usually portends that the out-party has very little chance of winning the presidential election.

We decided to use a party's nominating process for the presidency as the principal means of measuring harmony and conflict at national nominating conventions because the nomination of a candidate for the presidency is the primary function of such conventions.

The critical measuring device proposed by our model is the proportion of delegate votes received by the strongest candidate for the presidential nomination in each major party on the first ballot. It is argued that the strength of the strongest candidate on the first ballot is indicative of both the general mood of the convention and the direction in which the convention will be forced to proceed. If an incumbent president receives 100 percent of the delegate votes on the first ballot, a harmonious convention is indicated, one which, in some cases, is very conducive to victory by the in-party. If, on the other hand, an incumbent president receives only 55 percent of the delegate votes on the first ballot, there is obviously considerable opposition to his renomination, and such a situation is normally not conducive to victory by an in-party.

If the out-party nominee receives more than 60 percent of the delegate votes on the first ballot, it is usually, but certainly not always, an indication of a relatively harmonious convention. Such an indication normally does not augur well for the victory chances of the out-party in the general election. However, if the strongest candidate in the out-party receives between 50 and 60 percent of the delegate votes on the first ballot, a relatively high level of conflict within the party is usually indicated. Conflict in the out-party frequently acts as an energizing device and increases the probability that the party will win the general election. If the out-party's strongest candidate receives less than 50 percent of the delegate votes on the first ballot, however, the vote frequently indicates that the party is so split that it may not be capable of coalescing sufficiently around one candidate to produce the type of campaign needed to win the presidency.

TYPE A—THE CONCILIATORY CONVENTION

The most powerful type of nominating convention historically has been the type we refer to as a Type A or conciliatory convention. This type of convention is one in which the party does not have an incumbent running for the presidential nomination, and the strongest candidate receives between 50 and 59 percent of the delegate votes on the first ballot. Some of the most familiar Type A conventions were those held by the Democrats in 1932, when Franklin Roosevelt was nominated to run against the incumbent President Herbert Hoover, and by the Republicans in 1952, when General Dwight Eisenhower was nominated by the Republicans to run against Adlai Stevenson. In 1960 Senator John Kennedy was nominated by the Democrats in a Type A convention to run against then Vice President Richard Nixon, and in 1968 Richard Nixon was nominated by a Type A convention to run against then Vice President Hubert Humphrey.

The Type A or conciliatory convention offers an interesting blend of conflict and harmony. Generally there appears to be sufficient conflict in the Type A convention to provide the enthusiasm and vigor needed by the party to conduct a strenuous and successful campaign. But there also appears to be a high enough level of harmony to enable the party to unite around its strongest candidate and conduct a unified campaign that effectively holds both its own partisans and attracts more than its normal share of independent voters and new voters.

Until 1936, the Democratic party operated under a two-thirds rule in nominating its presidential candidate, that is, a candidate for the Democratic party's presidential nomination had to receive the votes of two-thirds of the delegates at the convention before the nomination could be tendered him. It is interesting to note that since 1864 only one candidate, Champ Clark, in 1912, received more than 50 percent of the delegate votes and failed to win the nomination. Despite this one experience, it has traditionally been the case with both major parties that if one candidate receives close to 50 percent of the votes on the first ballot he will not be denied the nomination. Since 1864, no candidate for the presidential nomination in either of the major parties who has received more than 41 percent of the delegate votes on the first ballot has failed to receive that party's presidential nomination, a good indication that the conventions normally act in a rational manner. If a candidate appears to have a fairly commanding lead and if his total delegate vote count is approaching the point at which he would receive the nomination, now 50 percent for both parties, the convention usually gives that candidate the nomination. In the fifty-four conventions held since 1864, only six candidates have received between 40 and 50 percent of the delegate votes on the first ballot, which suggests that if the candidate is strong enough to receive more than 40 percent of the delegate votes on the first ballot, he is usually strong enough to convince uncommitted delegates that he will receive the nomination and, therefore, gain many of their votes on the first ballot. This pattern of delegate support is one reason why the Type A nominee is so strong. No Type A nominee between 1864 and 1968 received fewer popular votes than his opponent.

The Type A nominee is apparently just strong enough to win the nomination but not strong enough to overwhelm the opposition. The Type A nominee's level of strength indicates, first of all, that he is supported by at least half of the delegates at the convention on the first ballot, usually a good indication that his nationwide strength is considerable. In addition, the Type A nominee has probably been forced to come to agreement with a number of state delegations and uncommitted delegations in order to bring them into his camp, and in the process, probably was compelled to moderate any extreme positions he might have held prior to coming to the convention. Possessing just 50 percent of the vote means also that there is little chance that the victorious nominee can control the platform deliberations so closely that a platform can be written which might not appeal to most factions of the party. Being just strong enough to win the nomination, the candidate could be compelled to accept platform planks that are not entirely consistent with his past positions.

Second, a Type A candidate, that is, one who received just over 50 percent of the delegate votes on the first ballot, was probably involved in a number of battles with other candidates for state delegations. With just over 50 percent of the delegates favoring one candidate on the first ballot, it is likely that there was considerable conflict among the delegations as a whole over who the best candidate would be for the party's nomination, as well as considerable struggling within the party prior to the convention. The preconvention and primary fight over just who will receive the nomination may be conducted with enthusiasm and vigor. As long as the contest over the nomination does not become too personal and does not denigrate the leading candidate so completely that it is difficult for him to win the November election, the enthusiasm and the heated contest for the nomination can be positive factors for the party.

Frequently, in a hotly contested battle for a party's nomination, the candidates involved in the battle receive considerable publicity from the nation's media. Publicity on television and radio and in newspapers normally tends to generate charisma and provide support for the candidates who prove themselves to be the strongest. The preconvention battles for the nomination focus the attention of media audiences on several of the candidates and make them national figures as they speak out on major issues. In marked contrast are campaigns in which there is little competition for the party's nomination and none of the candidates receive an exceptional public reception. If a candidate is running unopposed in a primary or is unopposed in his attempts to win a state's delegate votes, he normally gets little publicity. But if several candidates are competing for a state's delegate votes, all of the candidates will probably get some publicity, and the candidate who ends up on top, of course, will receive considerable publicity both state and nation wide.

To sum up, a Type A candidate has several advantages which make the probability of his winning the presidency extraordinarily high. Because of his low winning margin in the convention he is usually forced to moderate any extreme stances he might have been tempted to take. He is forced to make concessions to the other factions in the convention. He is not capable of railroading a platform through that might alienate or isolate factions within the party. And, in the hotly contested battles for the nomination which precede the convention he has won considerable national attention.

The first battle for the candidate is the battle to obtain the nomination. The candidate who wins a hotly contested nomination and receives just over 50 percent of the delegate votes on the first ballot is often perceived as the victor in a trial by fire. As such, he is assured of a more highly esteemed and more highly publicized place in the public eye than what he would have had if he had not weathered battles with other leaders in the party in his drive to win the nomination.

TYPE B CONVENTIONS

The Type B nominating convention is the second strongest type of nominating convention. Historically, the nominees of Type B conventions have always received more popular votes in presidential contests than their opponents, except when their opponent was the nominee of a Type A convention. The Type B convention is characterized by the party that has an incumbent president and is strongly unified behind him. The Type B convention is geared to continuing the administration of a chief executive and a political team that are already in power. The incumbent president wishes to be renominated, and a united party gives him that nomination.

Our formula defines a Type B nominee as one who is an incumbent president and receives more than 60 percent of the delegate votes on the first ballot. In reverse chronological order, the Type B candidates have been the following: President Lyndon Johnson in 1964 when he ran against Senator Barry Goldwater; President Dwight Eisenhower, who ran against Adlai Stevenson in 1956; President Harry Truman, who ran against Thomas Dewey in 1948; and President Franklin Roosevelt, who in 1944, 1940, and 1936 ran as a Type B candidate.

The following also ran as Type B candidates: President Coolidge in 1924 ran against John W. Davis; Woodrow Wilson in 1916 ran against Charles Evans Hughes; Theodore Roosevelt in 1904 ran against Alton B. Parker; William McKinley in 1900 ran against William Jennings Bryan; Grover Cleveland in 1888 ran against Benjamin Harrison; Ulysses S. Grant in 1872 ran against Horace Greeley; and Abraham Lincoln in 1864 ran against General George B. McClellan. The lowest percentage of delegate votes received by any of these incumbent presidents on their attempts to win renomination on the first ballot was the 78.3 percent received by incumbent President Harry Truman in 1948. Eight of these incumbent presidents received 100 percent of the delegate votes on the first ballot.

The Type B nominating convention can produce a very powerful political campaign machine. The Type B nominee is an incumbent president whose success in office is evidenced by the fact that the party has united to offer him a second try at the presidency. The nominee heads the vast and powerful machinery of government that is the singular perquisite of an incumbent president. The nominee also has the tremendous advantage of already being known by most of the voting population.

The Type B convention is characterized by harmony. The delegates support the president and usually accept without question his suggestions for party platform proposals. The president usually has considerable financial support and enjoys most of the advantages that can accrue to a political candidate.

Probably the major weakness of a Type B nominee, and one of the reasons why we rate a Type A nominee as stronger, is the lack of vigor and enthusiasm that can frequently characterize a president's attempt at re-election. Harmony is a prerequisite for the successful renomination of a president; at the same time, the lack of conflict within the nominating convention can be a considerable disadvantage to the candidate. If the opposition party has weathered considerable strife in reaching its nomination without generating acrimonious personal debate between the candidates but rather has focused attention on the weaknesses of the incumbent president, then the president's performance in office may become the center of considerable criticism and debate. He, at the same time, has nobody to provide him with the opportunity for consistent criticism of the opposition in a campaign-type atmosphere. An incumbent president must be careful of the level and extent of his criticism of opposing candidates. It is possible for a president's continued criticism of a leading contender for the opposition party's nomination to provide positive support to that candidate and undercut his own position in the long run.

It may require considerable effort on the part of an incumbent president to imbue his campaign forces with the type of energy and enthusiasm that frequently buoy up the forces of an opposition party attempting to topple the party in power. The president is thus caught in a rather difficult dilemma. On the one hand, he must maintain party harmony in order to consolidate his own position within the party; an absence of harmony within the controlling party is an even greater indication of weakness than is a stupefying plenitude of harmony.

On the other hand, the presence of complete harmony may be a serious disadvantage in that it does not give the president the same type of opportunities to strike out at his opponents that they have of striking out at him; it does not provide the same type of mechanisms to develop party enthusiasm and vigor that the out-party has after it has gone through a succession of hotly fought primary contests.

TYPE C CONVENTIONS

Type C conventions are generally held by a party which does not have an incumbent president seeking renomination but which gives more than 60 percent of its delegate votes to the strongest candidate on the first ballot. In 1964, Senator Barry Goldwater, a Type C candidate, ran against incumbent President Lyndon Johnson. In 1960 a Type C convention nominated Richard Nixon to run against Senator John Kennedy. In 1956 a Type C convention nominated Adlai Stevenson. Other candidates coming from Type C conventions were: Thomas Dewey in 1944, Governor Alfred Landon in 1936, Herbert Hoover and Alfred Smith in 1928, William Howard Taft and William Jennings Bryan in 1908, Alton B. Parker in 1904, William Jennings Bryan in 1900, Grover Cleveland in 1892, Horace Greeley in 1872, and Ulysses S. Grant in 1868.

At each of these conventions there was one candidate who was obviously the strongest contender. On the first ballot that strong figure received more than 60 percent of the delegate votes. Usually, the percentage received by the Type C candidate is considerably above 60 percent. Several of the candidates received nearly 100 percent; the lowest received by any candidate was the 66 percent received by Adlai Stevenson in 1956. Five of the Type C nominees received less than 70 percent of the delegate votes on the first ballot. A Type C candidate who receives nearly unanimous support on the first ballot is frequently the party's titular leader or someone who is acknowledged to be the party's only conceivable choice for the presidential nomination. There is normally little discussion about which candidate will win the nomination, because it is quite obvious from the beginning of the convention that one candidate has the nomination sewed up.

Although a Type C nominating convention can produce a strong candidate and a powerful campaign machine, it has several distinct disadvantages. These disadvantages stem from the presence of either too much harmony or too much conflict. The first of these disadvantages, and perhaps the most serious, is the possibility that the Type C nominee may receive more than 60 percent of the delegate votes but may not, at the same time, be able to unify the party around his candidacy. In this case the candidate may receive 70 percent of the vote, while the remaining 30 percent of the vote represents adamant opposition to his candidacy. The candidate in a Type A convention may be opposed by fairly large segments of the convention, but the fact that the candidate wins the nomination by a bare majority usually indicates that most factions of the party feel their candidates have lost a fair fight. Thus, they bow to the inevitable and accept the candidacy of the leader who gets more than 50 percent of the votes. The opponents of a Type C candidate may feel very differently. The Type C candidate frequently gets such a large percentage of the vote that he is not forced to moderate his stands vis-à-vis other factions in the party and, as a matter of fact, is frequently able to steamroller the convention into doing whatever he wishes. When the nominee is forced neither to moderate his extreme stances nor to make conciliatory gestures to opposing factional leaders, the Type C nominating convention may see segments of the party becoming isolated and alienated from the candidacy of the party's leader. Type C nominating conventions occasionally are troubled by threats to bolt the party by factions who feel that they have been snubbed, ignored, or, perhaps, alienated by the failure of a party leader to take their feelings into consideration.

The Type C convention not only offers the possibility that a leading political figure may alienate factions of his own party and, in turn, make electoral success in the general election very difficult, but it also creates an equally unfavorable condition of harmony in his party if his party is the out-party. An out-party nomination of a Type C candidate may indicate that the out-party is not in a very strong position vis-à-vis the national electorate. The lack of serious contenders for the presidential nomination may be a sign that the party has fared poorly in the latest elections for the United States Senate and the governorships of major states or that the nationwide fortunes of the party are on the downswing. A party that has not been successful in winning the governorships or the senatorships of large states is frequently a party that will not have many topflight candidates for the presidential nomination. Thus the door is open for one candidate to be accepted as the leader of the party and to sweep to an easy first-ballot nomination, but his chances of winning the presidency are slight.

The lack of a serious contest for the presidential nomination evidenced by a first-ballot vote of more than 60 percent for one candidate usually indicates also that the preconvention struggle for delegates has not been as intense as it would be in a Type A nominating convention. As a result, the Type C candidate's party normally does not conduct as vigorous and as forceful a presidential campaign as does the party of a Type A candidate.

Thus, the Type C nominee may be several steps behind at the very beginning of the presidential campaign. His nomination in a convention that does not exhibit the conflict normally associated with a Type A convention may indicate that some segments of his party are severely dissatisfied or alienated. The candidate chosen by an indifferent convention may not have been forced to make conciliatory gestures to the major segments of the party and may have been able to ram unpopular platform positions through the convention. Such a candidate has not been forced to compete in hotly contested preconvention drives to gain delegate votes and may remain relatively unknown without the extensive coverage normally accorded by the media to a candidate who has been victorious in contested preconvention battles. Last, but still important, the Type C nominating convention may result simply because the party is woefully weak and may, in fact, have chosen a candidate who under more auspicious times for the party would not be considered of presidential caliber. Candidates of presidential caliber may have decided, because the party's fortunes are at a low ebb, to wait until the party is on the upswing before they make an attempt to win their party's nomination.

TYPE D CONVENTIONS

Type D conventions are conventions in which the party does not have an incumbent and no candidate receives more than 50 percent of the delegate votes on the first ballot. Nominees of Type D conventions have been able to garner more popular votes than only two types of presidential nominees, Types E and F. Type D nominees have always received fewer popular votes in presidential contests than the nominees of Types A, B, or C conventions.

Type D conventions, which are referred to as compromise conventions, have become less frequent in recent years. Examples of Type D nominees would be Adlai Stevenson in 1952, Thomas Dewey in 1948, Wendell Willkie in 1940, John W. Davis in 1924, both Warren G. Harding and James Cox in 1920, Charles Evans Hughes in 1916, Woodrow Wilson in 1912, William Jennings Bryan in 1896, Benjamin Harrison in 1888, and Grover Cleveland in 1884. Both James A. Garfield and Winfield Scott Hancock in 1880, Rutherford B. Hayes in 1876, and Horatio Seymour in 1868 were Type D candidates.

The Type D convention can be a strong convention in terms of producing a unified party for the presidential campaign. Frequently, the forces that combine to produce a Type D convention indicate that a number of factions are struggling for the presidential nomination. The Type D convention normally tries to select a compromise candidate who is able to unify all of the warring factions and then enter the presidential campaign at the head of a cohesive and united party.

In contrast to a Type C convention, which is characterized by a strong leader who is generally accepted by most elements within the party, the Type D convention is characterized by the lack of a strong, dominating leader. Historically, Type D conventions have produced candidates for the presidency who were not the leading contenders for the party's nomination coming into the convention. All of the nation's dark-horse candidates have been the nominees of Type D conventions. Frequently, the party nominees from Type D conventions have received only a few votes on the first ballot. What has happened has been the surging to the fore of several strong candidates who proved unable to gain sufficient votes to win the nomination. As their candidacies collapsed, compromise candidates rushed forward in an attempt to bring together all the factions supporting the strong candidates who had faltered.

Type D conventions occurred quite frequently in years past, but the advanced polling techniques and the sophisticated delegate-counting capabilities of the present era have made compromise candidates the infrequent exception today. Nationwide polling makes it possible for all of the delegates to get a good idea of each available candidate's potential ability to defeat the opposition party's candidate. In years past, a compromise candidate might be one who today would pull a minuscule proportion of the nationwide sample taken to inform the delegates and, of course, the nation as a whole as to what the country's electorate is thinking. The compromise candidate was a candidate of political bosses and closed conventions in which a few men could meet and decide that a political figure known only to the members of his family and close friends would be the party's nominee for president, because the factions within the party had reached a stalemate.

The Type D convention can produce a candidate who has unifying capabilities for a party that is divided among several strong candidates. But this type of convention normally cannot produce the type of strong leader who emerges from the Type C convention.

The Type D convention may result because the party's fortunes are on the upswing as victories in state senatorial races and state gubernatorial races produce a number of strong candidates who then set their sights on the presidency.

But a D convention may also indicate the exact opposite. The party may be in such a weakened condition that only mediocre candidates are available to fight for the right to lead the party's ticket. The major reason the D convention is weaker than the C is the type of unity the D convention produces and the relative personal popularity of the nominees. The harmony produced by the D convention is the shallow unity derived from the general satisfaction of the major factions that their chief opponent did not win. They don't ordinarily go as far as Senator Silas Wright of New York did in 1844 when he refused the vice-presidential nomination because his candidate, Martin Van Buren, did not get the presidential nod, or bolt the party as they might have had their primary adversary won. But they do find it difficult to provide the wholehearted support they would have given to a man considered to be the party's top candidate. The frequent weakness of the D candidate, then, compounds the difficulty of generating vigorous unity within the party. If none of the party's top talent was able to excite enough support to receive a majority vote on the first ballot, the deep feeling of candidate weakness is difficult to surmount. The party normally rallies around its nominee, but the harmony is not as strong as that present at the C convention, where a nominee is accorded an almost unanimous vote on the first ballot, or at a B convention which returns an incumbent behind a unified party.

TYPE E CONVENTIONS

Type E conventions are characterized by a party with an incumbent president which nominates that incumbent president with less than 60 percent of the delegate votes on the first ballot. There have been two Type E conventions, that of 1912, when William Howard Taft received only 52 percent of the delegate votes on the first ballot to win the Republican renomination for president, and that of 1892 when Benjamin Harrison received only 58.6 percent of the delegate votes in his renomination attempt.

A Type E convention signifies considerable conflict within the in-party, a situation that in-parties try hard to avoid. The fact that the incumbent president can amass no more than 60 percent of the delegate votes on the first ballot is proof of considerable party dissatisfaction with his performance in office. The dissatisfaction of the president's own party with his performance in office is communicated to voters throughout the electorate, and it is difficult to expect a majority of them to support a candidate for re-election when his own party is hesitant to renominate him. Conflict within the president's own party and the lack of unity and cohesion it breeds are normally almost impossible to overcome in a presidential election. As a matter of fact, no nominee of a Type E convention has ever been re-elected to the presidency.

TYPE F CONVENTIONS

A Type F convention is a convention which is characterized by a party with an incumbent president whom it refuses to renominate even though that incumbent candidate wishes to be renominated. There has been only one Type F convention, and that was in 1884 when the Republican party refused to nominate Chester A. Arthur. Instead, it nominated James G. Blaine, who lost to Grover Cleveland, a compromise candidate for the Democratic party's nomination.

An interesting case occurred in 1868, when the incumbent president for the Republican party was actually a Democrat, Andrew Johnson, who had succeeded to the presidency upon Lincoln's assassination in 1865. Johnson had been taken on by Abraham Lincoln as his vice-presidential candidate in 1864 because his Democratic party ties were considered to be important in attracting Democrats to the Republican Lincoln. Johnson, knowing that he could not receive the Republican nomination because he was a Democrat, tried for the Democratic nomination but lost to Horatio Seymour. Inasmuch as Johnson was not the incumbent Democratic president, but rather the Democratic president of the incumbent Republican party, we did not consider the 1868 case to be a Type F convention. Thus 1884 is considered the only Type F convention.

A Type F convention is similar to a Type E convention, except that it provides an even weaker candidate than a Type E convention. If the party itself argues that its incumbent should not be renominated for the presidency, it is difficult to expect the nation's voters to return that party as a whole to power, regardless of who the party may nominate for its highest office.

Besides the general lack of national support for a party that has as much as admitted that its leader and the nation's chief executive failed to effectively lead the nation, the incumbent president always has a cadre of supporters who will be furious if he is denied another chance to win office. These supporters may comprise a considerable faction of the party, as they did in 1884. If their leader, the incumbent president, loses his bid for renomination, many of them stand to lose their jobs, and all of them stand to lose someone they hold in high esteem. This attachment to the sitting president is not to be taken lightly, and successful attempts to deny him renomination will almost certainly create serious breaches within the party. The new nominee is faced with a dual problem, then: he must convince the electorate that he should not be held responsible for the failings of the old president, and he must assuage the anger of the cohorts and followers of the party's deposed leader.

SIX CONVENTION STYLES SUMMARIZED

Between 1864 and 1968, four presidential elections were contested by candidates selected by the same type of party nominating convention. In 1880 both James Garfield and Winfield Scott Hancock were chosen by Type D conventions; both candidates were compromise candidates. In 1908 both William Howard Taft and William Jennings Bryan were selected by Type C conventions; in 1920 both Warren G. Harding and James Cox were selected by Type D conventions; and in 1928 both Herbert Hoover and Alfred Smith were the candidates of Type C conventions.

When a tie occurs, i.e., both major candidates are selected by the same type of convention, the outcome of the presidential election cannot be predicted accurately by use of the formula discussed earlier in this chapter. Our formula contends that if the candidates of both major parties were selected by party conventions of the same style, the conventions would tend to cancel each other out as influence mechanisms, because both parties would emerge from the convention process at similar levels of party cohesion and energy. A candidate nominated by a Type C convention would tend to inherit the same strengths and weaknesses from his convention that his opponent would have if he had also been nominated by a Type C convention.

By suggesting that the conventions do not have systematic influences on the electoral chances of the two major candidates when their parties have similar convention styles, we are not arguing that the conventions have no impact on the results of the election that year. We are simply arguing that the conventions do not have the same degree of systematic impact that one would expect them to have when there are different styles of conventions in competition with each other.

Another significant factor in understanding our general formula is our method of determining the outcome of the presidential contests. Of course, the president is not chosen by the people per se; rather he is selected by a small group of individuals who constitute what is known as the electoral college. We have measured the impact of the conventions on presidential elections not in terms of the electoral college vote but rather in terms of the popular vote.

We have taken this second route for several reasons. The first is that we feel the popular vote is a more accurate reflection of the feelings of the entire American electorate than is the voting in the electoral college. If one candidate receives a majority or a plurality of the votes of the entire American electorate but does not receive a majority of the votes in the electoral college, we feel that it is this candidate who received the greatest support through his nominating convention. Our feeling, then, is that Convention A was stronger than Convention B if Convention A candidates always received more popular votes than Convention B candidates. And Convention B was stronger than Convention C if Convention B candidates received more votes than Convention C candidates.

For our present purposes we have ignored the electoral vote because two exceptions exist to the general rule that candidates who receive the most popular votes win. Both in 1876 and in 1888 the candidate with the greatest number of popular votes lost. Therefore, any attempt to predict presidential election outcomes must be based on one of the two methods of measurement, either electoral votes or popular votes. We selected the popular vote as the base for our formula because we feel it most accurately reflects which political convention produced the greatest popular response for its candidate.

Another reason for using the popular vote count instead of the electoral vote count is that we feel the differences between electoral vote counts and popular vote counts are more or less a phenomenon of the past. No candidate since 1888 has received more popular votes than his opposition and not received more votes in the electoral college. We feel, therefore, that in order to be consistent we should use popular vote counts throughout our study. Using popular votes also eliminates the necessity of haggling over which campaign was really successful in 1876 and 1888, that which got the greatest number of popular votes or that which received the majority of the electoral votes.

We certainly do not feel that ours is the only way of evaluating presidential election outcomes. As a matter of fact, we welcome any alternative method of combining the two measuring procedures into one or arguments indicating why the electoral college outcome would be a more accurate reflection of the strength of American political party conventions.

In this chapter we have argued that the conventions of the major American political parties from 1864 through 1968 can be divided into six different types. Each of these types reflects in varying degrees the mood of the country and the condition of the nation's major political parties. We have also suggested that the style of convention produced by the major parties provides an indication of the probability that a particular nominee will receive more popular votes than his opponent.

The formula we have developed identifies six types of conventions, which we have designated A, B, C, D, E, and F. Type A is a convention in which one candidate receives more than 50 percent of the vote but less than 60 percent, and the incumbent president is not a contender for the nomination. Type B is a convention that has an incumbent president who is renominated with more than 60 percent of the delegate votes on the first ballot. Type C conventions are those in which there is no incumbent president and the strongest candidate receives more than 60 percent on the first ballot. The Type D convention is characterized by the lack of an incumbent president and the failure of any candidate to receive more than 50 percent of the delegate votes on the first ballot. Types E and F are conventions in which an incumbent president receives less than 60 percent of the vote. The Type E convention renominates its incumbent president with a bare majority, but the Type F convention frustrates the attempt of the sitting president to lead his party's ticket and nominates someone else to carry the party's banner.

CHAPTER FOUR

1932
Roosevelt vs. Hoover
TYPE A VS. TYPE B

On Thursday, June 14, 1928, John L. McNab nominated Herbert Hoover for president of the United States. McNab declared that Hoover was not only a great engineer but also a great humanitarian. He called Hoover the creature of his age and said that in many respects the age would reflect Hoover, which was a rather unfortunate way of placing blame for the nation's longest and most severe depression upon the shoulders of Herbert Hoover.

By 1932 most of the nation's political watchers, and probably most American citizens, were assuming that the depression was so all-pervasive that the Republicans were certain to lose in the November elections. So the Republicans went to their convention in Chicago faced with the task of nominating a candidate who could lead the party only to certain defeat. There was little doubt in anyone's mind that the party would lose with Herbert Hoover as the candidate. Slight as the chances were of the Republicans winning with Hoover, the party was assured of complete defeat without him. As was discussed in the previous chapter, one of the surest ways of guaranteeing a candidate's defeat is to refuse to renominate an incumbent president or to nominate an incumbent president with a disunited party. It seems clear that an incumbent president has done a poor job of administering the country when even his own party is reluctant to give him a second chance.

According to the formula we have developed, Herbert Hoover had three opportunities as far as his nomination was concerned. He could have been nominated by a Type B convention, a convention in which an incumbent president is renominated by more than 60 percent of the delegate votes on the first ballot. He could have been a Type E nominee, an incumbent president who is renominated with support from fewer than 60 percent of the delegates on the first ballot. Or, he could have participated in a Type F convention, that is, one in which he is not renominated at all. Republican party leaders in 1932 were sufficiently aware of political party history in the United States to know that the party had suffered defeat in 1884, 1892, and 1912, when it had refused to renominate an incumbent president or had nominated an incumbent president with less than a united party. In 1884 incumbent President Chester A. Arthur was denied renomination and the party turned to James G. Blaine, who lost to a Democrat, Grover Cleveland. In 1892 incumbent President Benjamin Harrison received only 58.6 percent of the delegate votes on the first ballot, making him the nominee of a Type E convention, and Harrison lost to Grover Cleveland in the November election. In 1912 when William Howard Taft received the votes of only 52 percent of the delegates on the first ballot, he went on to lose to Woodrow Wilson in the November election.

The party leaders knew that, regardless of how poorly the country had fared from 1929 through 1932, if the party were to abandon its incumbent, it would stand an even smaller chance of winning the presidency than it would if it stuck by its president. The party leaders doubtless also knew that no incumbent since 1864 had ever received fewer popular votes than his opponent when he was renominated by a united party. So, in 1932, Herbert Hoover was renominated for president of the United States by the Republican party and given 98 percent of the delegate votes on the first ballot. The party leaders anticipated a loss in 1932. But they felt that by renominating Hoover they could show a united front and hoped that the Democrats, who were engaged in severe intraparty squabbles, would tear themselves apart and in the process lose the election.

The fact that a united front formed around President Hoover should not be taken as an indication that there was no opposition to his candidacy. In fact, there was serious and extensive opposition to the president's renomination. One group wanted to nominate former President Calvin Coolidge, who had been out of office since 1929. But Coolidge remained silent, giving his supporters no hope. Joseph I. France of Maryland was not a serious candidate for the presidency, but he entered a number of primaries just to show that there was serious popular opposition to President Hoover. He won a number of these primaries.

But most of the party leaders including Senators Borah, Hiram Johnson, George Norris, Robert La Follette, Jr., and Frank Lowden, even though they might have realized that Hoover did not stand a chance, probably knew also that no other Republican leader stood much of a chance either. They were content then to sit back and allow Hoover to be renominated simply because they felt that it was the only expedient thing to do. They expected to lose in 1932, and evidently they felt that a united loss in 1932 would be better for the party than a divisive loss.

The advantages of incumbency and, thus, the advantages of being nominated by a Type B convention are defined in terms of money, attention, organization, and experience. The president who has a united party behind him is a very difficult man to beat in an election. He has had four years of free publicity given to him by the nation's mass media. He has thousands of jobs to dispense to the party faithful. He has a nationwide organization, which proved its ability when he won the presidency. And he has the advantage of saying to the American people that he has been the president for four years and he knows how the job must be done.

Incumbency also generates disadvantages. The incumbent frequently lacks the enthusiasm and the vitality of his challenger. He has been in office for four years, and he has grown rather accustomed to the perquisites of the office and the decision-making power that he possesses. He is not accustomed to lashing out at his opponents; rather he is accustomed to defending his own proposals from the slashing attacks of those who would like to take his place. It is a rare president who has not disappointed someone during his four years in office. He is usually unable to fulfill all of his promises and almost inevitably there are those who feel that the president has not lived up to their expectations.

The challenger has the advantages of enthusiasm, righteous indignation, and of not yet having been in a position to disappoint the expectations of a nationwide group of followers. The challenger can attack the president for not fulfilling the great expectations of his office; he can argue that the president's experience is not necessarily an advantage, but, as in the case of President Hoover, a severe disadvantage, for the president was obviously not able to cope with the nation's economic problems.

In the 1932 contest there was on one side an incumbent President Herbert Hoover, renominated by a united party with 98 percent of the delegate votes on the first ballot. Hoover was a candidate who possessed the advantages of the incumbency, such as they were in 1932, and a candidate who ran knowing that no incumbent president since 1864 had been defeated when he was renominated by a united party.

But it was also true in 1932 that no incumbent president or nominee of a Type B convention had ever run against a nominee of a Type A convention. So President Hoover in 1932 was to be the first Type B nominee to run against a Type A nominee, who according to our formula is the nominee of the most powerful type of political convention. Herbert Hoover was nominated in 1932 by a united party, but a party that exhibited the exaggerated effects of the Type B convention. It was a convention which nominated its candidate almost without enthusiasm. A serious divisiveness among the Republicans was smoothed over by a concern for unity and a firm conviction on the part of many that the congressional elections of 1930 were a nationwide indication of extreme dissatisfaction with the Republican party.

Franklin Delano Roosevelt ran as a Type A candidate. Several characteristics of the Type A nominating convention make it an extremely powerful nominating convention and give the presidential nominee an exceptional opportunity to win the presidency. The Type A convention, which nominates a candidate on the first ballot with between 50 and 59 percent of the vote when there is no party incumbent, indicates that a number of strong candidates within the party are competing for the party's presidential nomination.

This serious struggle for the nomination is a good indication that a number of powerful politicians feel that there is a good chance of winning the presidency, and that the party has probably been relatively successful in the last congressional election. In 1932 that was certainly the case with the Democrats. In 1928 the Republicans held 267 House seats and the Democrats 167; in 1930 the Democrats took control of the House of Representatives with 220 seats to 214 seats for the Republicans. Between the 1928 presidential election and the 1930 off-year election, the Democrats had gained a total of 53 seats in the House of Representatives.

The nominee of a Type A convention is a strong candidate because as the victor in the competition for the party's nomination, he has become the focus of national attention. When a number of contenders are vying for a major party's presidential nomination, the media usually give considerable attention to the contest, whereas contests in which there is little competition receive much less attention. If one candidate is able to rise above the others in this sometimes extended and almost always heated competition, that candidate is immediately singled out by the press for special attention. This special attention normally invests the candidate with a certain amount of charisma. Therefore, the candidate of a Type A nomination is usually a much more publicized candidate and frequently a much more charismatic candidate than the Type C nominee, who is the overwhelming favorite of his party and has been spared an extended and severe competition for the nomination.

The small majority with which the Type A candidate wins the nomination is also a good indication that he has not been able to steamroller the convention. If the candidate receives just over 50 percent of the votes on the first ballot, he has probably been forced to moderate his stances and make conciliatory gestures to other factions within the party. The need to conciliate factions was especially acute in the Democratic party prior to 1936, the year the Democratic party abolished the two-thirds rule,

which required that a candidate receive two-thirds of the votes
of the convention delegates to win the nomination.

The moderating forces that are usually operating in Type
A nominating conventions were clearly apparent in the Democratic platform of 1932. Even with the nation in the most
depressed economic state in its history, the Democrats were able
to produce a platform that promised to reduce government
expenditures by 25 percent and strongly favored a balanced
budget. The Democratic platform called for sound currency and
opposed the cancellation of debts owed the government by
foreign nations. It advocated unemployment and old age in-
surance under state laws, proposed price supports for farm
commodities, and strongly supported the repeal of prohibition.
All these planks in the platform were relatively mild stances to
adopt in the context of such a serious economic depression.

The contest for the Democratic presidential nomination in
1932 was fierce. The Democrats probably felt just as strongly as
the Republicans that 1932 would be a disastrous year for the
Republicans. It was, therefore, widely accepted in Democratic
circles that the Democratic nominee, whoever he might be,
would probably be the next president of the United States.

The three major contestants for the Democratic nomination
were Al Smith, former governor of New York, who had been
the Democratic nominee in 1928 and who had been defeated by
Herbert Hoover; John Nance Garner, the 61-year-old Speaker
of the House from Texas; and Franklin D. Roosevelt, the governor of New York. Roosevelt began to distinguish himself as the
candidate to beat in 1932 by winning the governorship of New
York in 1928, while presidential candidate Al Smith was losing
that state to Herbert Hoover. In 1930, Roosevelt was re-elected
by an overwhelming majority of 725,000 votes, carrying even
the Republican areas of upstate New York.

The primaries were hotly contested in 1932, and the lead see-
sawed back and forth, even though during most of this period
Roosevelt was considered the man with the inside track to the
presidency. His losses in Massachusetts and California slowed
his bandwagon somewhat, but in the end his only serious opposition came from the former presidential candidate, Al Smith.

The 1932 convention battle turned out to be so intense that the Democrats approached the point of self-destruction. The conflict between Smith and Roosevelt grew so severe that it was feared the Democrats might do to themselves what everyone was certain the Republicans could not do, that is, defeat themselves. In the end Roosevelt received the nomination; John Nance Garner became his vice-presidential nominee, and Al Smith left the convention a bitter man determined to offer no active support in the upcoming campaign of Franklin Roosevelt.

The campaign itself was highlighted by the defensive nature of Hoover's campaign and by the aggressive, innovative organization put together by Roosevelt. His brain trusters provided the speeches and Roosevelt himself provided much of the energy as he campaigned from coast to coast, moving across the nation by train to prove that his health, the issue with which the Republicans were attempting to defeat him, was not a serious factor in the campaign. Hoover did not really begin his campaign until October, and then his primary thrust was an attempt to convince the voters that recovery was just around the corner but that it would be sabotaged if the Democrats were voted into office. Hoover attacked Roosevelt on the tariff issue, and he alleged that the Democrats were little better than socialists. But in 1932 the threat of socialism fell on rather deaf ears in the bread lines.

Roosevelt criticized Hoover for his deficit budget and promised that he would balance the budget. He concentrated on farm policy, arguing for farm supports and more public power. Franklin Roosevelt was frequently backed into a corner by not being able to produce detailed estimates on how much his proposed changes in government policy would cost. Even one of his own brain-trusters, Rexford G. Tugwell, suggested that the candidate had no realistic view of the probable costs of his advocated policies.

All in all, it was a campaign that exemplified to a rather exaggerated degree the advantages and disadvantages of Type A and Type B conventions. Hoover had behind him a party united on the surface but divided underneath. Voters who were dissatisfied with his performance in office were hardly in a mood to manifest the enthusiasm that wins presidential contests. The great disadvantage of the Type B convention, its lack of vitality and enthusiasm, was exaggerated in 1932 and further weakened the position of Hoover, who probably would have been defeated under almost any conditions.

As we indicated earlier, convention style is simply a reflection of the dominant political feeling at a particular point in time. The lack of enthusiasm in the 1932 Republican campaign and the mode of renomination of President Hoover are good indications that even within the mainstream of Republican voters there was general agreement that President Hoover could not be re-elected. Convinced that their incumbent president could not win re-election, partly leaders were unable to motivate the normal party supporters to put forth a winning effort.

In contrast, the Democratic convention of 1932 reflected the exaggerated advantages given to the nominee of a Type A convention. The candidate has the advantage of gaining nationwide attention during the battle in which he has defeated his party opponents. Because of the factionalism in the party, the Type A nominee is forced to produce a moderate platform and to attempt to reconcile factional differences. Frequently the nominee's efforts result in a unified party, one made vigorous and enthusiastic by the struggle from which it has just emerged.

Franklin Roosevelt, who came into the 1932 convention as a factional leader, received more than 50 percent of the delegate votes on the first ballot. Once having received the nomination, he was able to unify almost all elements of the party into a structured organization that was capable of channeling the tremendous vitality built up through the primaries into the race for the presidency. The Type A nominee also has the advantage of being on the offensive. He can continue the critique of the president's performance as chief executive, which he began in the primaries, and carry it through to the general election. The president, on the other hand, usually must stand on his record and argue that his experience in office and his performance entitle him to a second term. Thus, we have enthusiasm, vitality, and an offensive posture versus experience, organization, publicity, lessened enthusiasm, and a defensive posture.

Some scholars would probably argue that 1932 was a unique case in that President Hoover was unusually susceptible to defeat. Certainly, we could not argue against that. But we would contend that the styles of the 1932 conventions probably are indicative of the difficulty that Hoover faced. When the president is considered strong and his chances for renomination are considered outstanding, there is probably very little chance that the opposition party would mount a Type A convention. When a Type A convention is opposed to a Type B convention, the nominee of the Type A convention probably must be given a slight advantage, because the level of the factional struggle preceding the Type A convention suggests that many of the strongest political leaders of the out-party believe the incumbent president to be vulnerable. Usually, this belief in the incumbent's vulnerability is based either on opinion data or on negative evaluations of the president's performance in office. It is highly unlikely that a Type A convention will unfold unless some weakness exists in the incumbent's record that encourages successful politicians of the out-party to believe he can be defeated. The competition for what promises to be a valuable nomination provides the core of vitality and enthusiasm that marks the Type A convention.

CHAPTER FIVE

1968
Nixon vs. Humphrey
TYPE A VS. TYPE C

In late August 1968, the Democratic party held its thirty-fifth national nominating convention in Chicago, Illinois. This convention nominated incumbent Vice-President Hubert Humphrey for the presidency, and in the process destroyed the presidential hopes of Hubert Humphrey. Humphrey failed to gain the exposure normally accorded a presidential nominee, and lost the support of several factions alienated by the bitterness of the convention proceedings.

Richard Nixon won the presidency in 1968, but the Democratic party won 51 more congressional seats than the Republicans. In recent history, the only other instance in which a candidate of one party won the presidency while his party was losing a significant number of congressional seats was in 1956 when incumbent President Dwight Eisenhower won re-election, but the Democrats won 33 more congressional seats than the Republicans.

Contrary to the expectations of many Republicans, the 1968 election did not signify a dramatic across the board repudiation of Democrats and return to Republicanism. George Gallup reported in his October 1968 summary that considerable dissatisfaction with the country's incumbent administration existed nationwide. Gallup reported a 60-year-old Wheeling, West Virginia, housewife as reflecting the angry and frustrated mood of the electorate in October of 1968 when she said, "This country is going to pot. We're not doing anything about the hippies, the yippies, and all the trouble in the cities. I wish I knew where we're headed."

"We can't be a lot worse off than we are now," said one middle-aged, blue-collar worker reflecting the views of many Democrats. "So why not try the change?"

Gallup suggested that, "The desire for a change in the nation's direction is probably the most potent single force in the thinking of the electorate at the moment."

But the Democrats were not thrown entirely out of office because the change Gallup saw a demand for in October of 1968 was not reflected in the congressional elections of 1968. American voters did not see the necessity for turning the congressional Democrats out and by a rather overwhelming majority returned them to power in Congress. After the 1968 elections, the Democrats controlled the House of Representatives with 243 seats to 192 for the Republicans, and the Senate with 57 seats to 43 for the Republicans. Richard Nixon did not win the election of 1968 because the nation's electorate was tired of the Democrats; he won for other reasons. Probably foremost among the other reasons for Nixon's victory was the divisive and embattled Democratic nominating convention in which the party tore itself apart amid a flood of negative publicity. The Republican convention, on the other hand, was more ridden by conflict than it appeared to be on the surface, but it was conflict of the type that can promote vitality and enthusiasm within the party. The conflict within the Republican party was capable of being transmuted into unity upon the close of the convention; thus it was a conflict that contributed to the Republican victory.

Like Adlai Stevenson, who was saddled with the burden of an unpopular administration in 1952, Hubert Humphrey was seen as the spokesman of an administration that had propelled the nation into an unpopular war. The vice-president was seen as a principal defender of the administration's policies of the preceding four years. Richard Nixon, on the other hand, was the leader of the out-party. He could argue quite persuasively, since he was backed by most of the nationwide polls, that the American people had rarely had it so bad. The United States was involved in an unpopular war. Crime and violence—especially the violence that had erupted in the ghetto areas of many of the nation's largest cities during the preceding three years—was directly attributed to the administration represented by Hubert Humphrey. Thus, the Democratic nominee, Hubert Humphrey, found himself not only on the defensive but also the nominee of a divided party. Richard Nixon, the Republican nominee, not only was on the offensive as the leader of the out-party, but also was the nominee of a united party. These factors were probably crucial in determining the outcome of the 1968 presidential election inasmuch as Nixon was able to defeat Humphrey, even though Republicans went down to resounding defeat in congressional elections throughout the nation.

The Republican convention of 1968 gave Richard Nixon many of the same advantages that the Democratic convention of 1932 had given Franklin Roosevelt. The 1968 Republican convention was a Type A convention, just like the Democratic convention of 1932. In 1932 Franklin Roosevelt received 57.7 percent of the delegate votes on the first ballot, giving him the nomination in a conciliatory convention. We discussed in Chapter 4 the advantages of vitality, enthusiasm, and unity that accrued to Roosevelt from this convention. The Republican convention of 1968 nominated Richard Nixon on the first ballot with 51.9 percent of the delegate votes.

Most of the political commentary describing the Republican convention of 1968 indicated that Richard Nixon was a virtual shoo-in for the nomination, and even after the convention there seemed to be a general agreement that Richard Nixon had won the nomination rather easily. Actually, the Republican convention of 1968 was a very faction-dominated convention, and Richard Nixon squeezed through to a 1.9 percent margin on the first ballot. Nixon came much closer to not receiving the Republican nomination in 1968 than most people realize.

As we mentioned in Chapter 3, a narrow victory plus the conflict that precedes the victory can be a tremendous advantage in the campaign that follows. Nixon's narrow victory on the first ballot indicated to the other factions in the convention that it had been a fair fight, that everyone had had his opportunity, and that Richard Nixon had squeezed through to a first-ballot victory. It was, therefore, relatively easy for his opponents to rally round and support his candidacy, because they felt that they had had their opportunity and that the best man had won. Nixon's 51.9 percent was not an overwhelming victory, and it indicated that even though support for the nominee was there, the support was not so overwhelming that the nominee could steamroller the convention, as Humphrey did a month later at the Democratic convention.

Hubert Humphrey was burdened by a convention that nominated him so overwhelmingly that his nomination was considered unfair by his opponents. Humphrey had no primary victories to his credit, so for him to receive two-thirds of the delegate votes without winning a single primary was considered not only undemocratic but also overwhelmingly unjust. The resentment of Humphrey's opponents at what they considered lack of fair play made it difficult for them to support his platform proposals or to rally round him after the convention was over. It generated conflict, which detracted from the publicity normally accruing to the presidential nominee, and it made it difficult for Humphrey to arouse the enthusiasm and vitality that are needed by a political party to win a presidential election.

In sharp contrast to the Democratic convention in Chicago in 1968, the Republican convention in Miami Beach nominated Richard Nixon with a bare majority. There was no general consensus among the Republicans as to who the party nominee should be, and Richard Nixon, mustering 51.9 percent of the delegates' support, just barely captured the nomination on the first ballot. His slight majority made it necessary for Nixon to compromise with various factions within the party, which, in turn, produced a convention that did not leave any significant elements of the party feeling alienated. Nixon was forced to moderate any extreme stances that he might have contemplated taking, in addition to providing a platform that could unify the various factions behind his candidacy. This conflict and re-unification around an accepted party leader generated the interesting combination of conflict and harmony that sets the

Type A convention apart from the others and gives it the necessary ingredients for a general election victory.

The Republican convention of 1968 was characteristic of Type A conventions. It exhibited a significant amount of conflict before the convention began between several factions struggling to gain the presidential nomination. The Type A convention, as exemplified by the 1968 Republican convention, shows a narrow victory on the first ballot by the party's strongest contender. In 1968 Richard Nixon received 51.9 percent of the delegate votes on the first ballot, an indication that his strength within the party was not overwhelming. In a Type A convention the platform must be acceptable to the various factions within the party, because the presidential nominee does not have the strength to steamroller a platform through, a process that could alienate factions the candidate may need at a later stage in the convention. With a bare majority of the vote, the strongest contender is not in a position to alienate even small factions. The narrow victory is also an advantage in that the factions that do not receive the nomination perceive the narrow victory as a just victory for the leading contender and as a fair defeat for themselves. Because they feel that they have fought the good fight and lost, they are willing to unite behind the nominee. This willingness to close ranks makes possible a unifying and forceful coalition behind the nominee's presidential campaign. The conflict existing within the convention prior to the nomination is also a very invigorating force for the party when it arouses the enthusiasm and vitality the party needs in order to win the November election. The constructive enthusiasm generated by the conflict within the 1968 Republican convention is a good indication of the type of constructive vitality a Type A convention can inject into a presidential campaign.

The Nixon campaign in 1968, following a Type A nomination, had money, organization, and a generally united party in the aftermath of a fair convention. The nominating convention and the campaign that followed indicated that Republicans across the country were unified behind their party's strongest candidate and were determined to wrest the presidency from the Democrats. Even though the Republicans did not have the widespread depth of support that was required to capture Congress, they were able to translate the enthusiasm and unity exemplified in their convention into a victory in the November elections.

In contrast, the Democratic convention of 1968 is a good indication of the severe disadvantages that accrue to the nominee of a Type C convention. Vice-President Hubert Humphrey was the nominee of a party that held almost a 2-1 lead in registered voters over its opposition. Humphrey, as the incumbent vice-president, had received a significant amount of publicity. In fact, Hubert Humphrey as an individual was known by somewhat more than 90 percent of America's voters. But Hubert Humphrey was nominated by a Type C convention, a type of convention that may indicate severe problems within the party.

A Type C convention is a convention in which no incumbent president is running for the nomination (President Johnson had stepped aside in late March 1968, indicating that he would not be a candidate for the party's nomination for a second full term in office) and in which the nominee who is the strongest contender for the presidential nomination receives more than 60 percent of the delegate votes on the first ballot. This type of convention is referred to as a steamroller convention. This steamroller quality is one of the disadvantages to a candidate of the Type C convention.

At the 1968 convention, Hubert Humphrey received 67.2 percent of the delegate votes on the first ballot. Humphrey had not won a single primary victory in 1968, whereas his principal rivals, Senators Eugene McCarthy of Minnesota and Robert Kennedy of Massachusetts, had battled throughout the spring to win delegates from the states that held presidential primaries. Humphrey refrained from entering these primaries, choosing instead to concentrate his attention on winning the delegate votes from states that selected delegates by other methods. When Humphrey received 67.2 percent of the delegate votes on the first ballot without winning a single primary victory, a large number of Democrats throughout the country felt that there was something inherently unfair about his nomination. How could the Democratic party nominate for the presidency a candidate who had failed to win even a single primary victory, while his principal opponent, Eugene McCarthy, had won several primary victories but was accorded only a minuscule proportion of the delegate votes?

The feeling of unfairness permeated the entire convention, and the dissatisfaction persisted among a large number of dissident Democratic leaders and, apparently, among large numbers of Democrats who failed to turn out on election day. The size of the Humphrey majority on the first ballot also indicated that he had the strength to steamroller through platform proposals that were unacceptable to large segments of the party. Because he knew he had a comfortable margin of victory, Vice-President Humphrey was able to push through a platform that did not criticize the administration's conduct of the war in Vietnam, even though at this stage George Gallup reported that by a margin of 53 percent to 35 percent, the American people believed that the United States had made a mistake in entering the fighting in Vietnam.

The feeling of unfairness associated with a steamroller convention alienates some party members from the general party platform and party direction and persuades them that their party lacks the enthusiasm and vitality exhibited by the candidate and the party of a Type A convention.

CHAPTER SIX

1952
Eisenhower vs. Stevenson
TYPE A VS. TYPE D

The 1952 preconvention campaigns and the 1952 Republican nominating convention exemplified the advantages that a Type A nominating convention provides. The Republican party had recovered quickly from the upset victory by Harry Truman over Thomas Dewey in 1948 and had made considerable gains in the mid-term elections of 1950. By 1952 Republicans across the country felt that the year had come for a Republican victory, the first Republican victory since 1928, when Herbert Hoover was elected president. The confidence that 1952 would be a successful presidential election year for the Republicans was reflected both in the intensity of the Republican contest for the presidency and in the number of candidates running in preconvention primaries in an effort to acquire the delegates necessary to win the Republican presidential nomination.

Type A presidential nominating conventions are frequently those of a party that has made substantial gains in the preceding congressional elections. In the congressional elections preceding the Republican Type A nominating convention in 1968, the Republicans picked up forty-seven congressional seats. In the congressional elections preceding the Democratic Type A nominating convention of 1960, the Democrats picked up fifty congressional seats. And in the congressional elections preceding the Type A Republican nominating convention of 1952, the Republicans picked up twenty-eight congressional seats. In the congressional elections preceding the 1932 Democratic Type A convention, the Democrats added fifty-three congressional seats, and in the congressional elections that preceded the Type A Democratic convention of 1876, the Democrats gained seventy-one additional congressional seats.

The resurgence of party strength in the preceding congressional election indicates that the party that has a Type A nominating convention is improving its general position at the polls and that it has an abundance, or at least a significant number, of strong candidates able to lead the party. If a party has suffered a number of disastrous congressional defeats, it will be difficult for it to find a significant number of nationally known candidates of presidential caliber who will fight in the preconvention primaries to determine who gets the presidential nomination.

The Republicans had done very well in the 1950 congressional elections, and by 1952 a number of nationally known Republicans were vying for the right to represent their party in the presidential election. The Republicans felt that their party was on the ascendant. They also felt that the Democratic party was in an extremely vulnerable position. The country was bogged down in a war in Korea; the Republicans had the country looking for Communists under every bed; and there were enough instances of corruption in the Truman administration to make that a viable campaign issue. So by 1952, the Republicans had a significant number of national level candidates, the party was on the ascendant, judging from the previous congressional elections, and the party had the three issues of communism, corruption, and Korea.

Because the moderate, internationalist eastern wing of the Republican party, which had captured the Republican nominations in 1940, 1944, and 1948, had lost each time, the old guard, led by Senator Robert A. Taft of Ohio, was determined that the nomination would not escape them again in 1952. In late 1951 Senator Taft launched his third major attempt to win the Republican nomination for the presidency by announcing that he would be a candidate in the Wisconsin primary. He argued that "Me-tooism" had led to three defeats on the part of the Republicans. Taft argued that the large numbers of new voters entering the electoral arena were looking for an alternative to the Democrats, with whom they were dissatisfied, rather than a candidate who would simply mirror the stances of the Democratic incumbents.

The leading candidate against Taft was General Dwight David Eisenhower, who was at the time the NATO commander in Paris. Eisenhower denied that he was interested in being a candidate at first. He suggested in November of 1951, however, that he might accept a draft as the Republican nominee. In December of 1951, Harold Stassen announced that he too was a bona fide candidate for the Republican nomination for the presidency. But Stassen in 1952 was hardly the liberal, golden boy of 1940 or the tremendously successful campaigner of the spring of 1948. He announced his candidacy by coming out solidly for old-fashioned honesty and "a solid dollar anchored to a modern gold standard." The Stassen campaign of 1952, like his later campaigns, was taken seriously by few people. The other major active candidate was Governor Earl Warren of California, who was then in his third term as governor. Warren expected to gain most of his support from party members who felt that Senator Taft was too conservative and General Eisenhower too recent a Republican. He entered only the California primary and based all of his chances for success on the expected deadlock between Taft and Eisenhower. He saw himself as a potential compromise candidate between the two major contenders.

The Republican convention exhibited all of the classical characteristics of a Type A convention: the party was on the upswing; it had done well in the previous congressional elections; it believed that the incumbent party was primed for defeat; it had at least two major contenders for the nomination; and it had witnessed a series of intense primary battles during which the party received considerable publicity and the victorious candidates in the primary elections were invested with the peculiar type of charisma generated by contemporary mass media. The conflict generated by the preconvention primaries and preconvention maneuvering could later be turned into a vital force to help propel the party toward victory in the November election.

A classical Type A convention would see the preconvention

primary generating conflict between at least two major candidates. The conflict would be resolved at the convention with one of the two major candidates receiving a bare majority on the first ballot and the second candidate then agreeing that it had been a fair battle and throwing all of his support behind the candidate to provide a unified front for the campaign. The vitality, the enthusiasm, and the hope generated during the preconvention proceedings could then be molded into a successful campaign machine which could, in turn, bring victory to the party.

In contrast to the Republicans' Type A convention, the Democrats were burdened with a Type D convention, that is, one in which the party has no incumbent running for renomination and the strongest contender receives less than 50 percent of the delegate votes on the first ballot. In the Democratic case in 1952, the strongest contender on the first ballot was Senator Estes Kefauver of Tennessee. Kefauver received 340 votes, or 27.7 percent, on the first ballot. Adlai Stevenson had 273, Richard Russell 268, Averell Harriman 123½, and ten other contenders split the remainder.

The weaknesses of the Type D convention are similar to the strengths of the Type C convention. But the weaknesses of the Type C convention provide the main strengths of the Type D convention. The Type C convention has a strong party leader who receives a significant amount of attention and publicity as the potential leader of the party, whereas the Type D convention is a convention without a strong party leader.

The Type C convention is characterized by a party forerunner who is so strong and so assured of the nomination that he is able to push through the convention a platform and convention procedure that suit his wishes but which may, in turn, alienate factions of the party. The Type D convention, on the other hand, is characterized by an almost leaderless party, a party that is forced to compromise on almost all issues simply because no one faction is significantly stronger than the other factions. The Type D convention is the convention of the smoke-filled room in which the bosses agree on a compromise candidate who can appeal to all elements within the party.

In the 1952 preconvention primaries only Senator Kefauver entered a significant number of primaries. The other candidates, like Senator Russell of Georgia, tended to limit themselves to one or two of the major primaries. Only Senator Kefauver, therefore, came into the convention with a significantly high level of nationwide popularity. The public opinion polls preceding the 1952 convention indicated that Kefauver had three to four times as much popular support as Governor Adlai Stevenson of Illinois. But regardless of the fact that Kefauver had won delegate votes in the New Hampshire, Wisconsin, Maryland, Florida, Ohio, Oregon, California, and South Dakota primaries, he was not the dominant figure at the 1952 Democratic national convention, and he never had a serious chance of winning the nomination. The 1952 convention was controlled by President Truman and various political bosses in the Northeast, the South, and the Midwest. Governor Stevenson was the favorite of only about 12 percent of the nation's Democrats prior to the 1952 Democratic nominating convention, but he was President Truman's favorite and the favorite of a number of the other important party bosses.

While a Type C nominee receives extensive publicity as the party leader and the obvious choice on the first ballot, and the Type A nominee receives significant attention because he has proven his mettle against the best that the party has to offer by winning in the primaries, the Type D nominee is frequently not well known to the majority of the nation's electorate. In the case of Adlai Stevenson, only about 12 percent of the nation's Democrats favored him as their presidential nominee. The vast plurality of the nation's Democrats supported Senator Kefauver of Tennessee. But at the convention it became quite obvious that Governor Stevenson was not only the choice of President Truman, but also the choice of many of the party bosses. Therefore, it became obvious very early in the balloting that Governor Stevenson would be the party's nominee. Thus, the wishes of the largest proportion of the nation's Democrats that Estes Kefauver be the party's nominee were ignored. Also, because Adlai Stevenson did not receive nationwide attention as the party's leader until after the Democratic convention, he was given only about three and a half months to capture the nation's attention, something General Eisenhower had already been doing for several years.

On Sunday, January 6, 1952, Senator Henry Cabot Lodge formally announced the Eisenhower candidacy by entering the General's name in the New Hampshire primary. In doing this, Lodge assured the nation, "that General Eisenhower is in to the finish." Eisenhower also announced that he was indeed willing to be drafted but that he would not seek the nomination actively. He said, "Under no circumstances will I ask for relief from this assignment [as NATO commander] in order to seek nomination to political office and I shall not participate in the preconvention activities of others who may have such intention with respect to me." The nation's electorate was not certain that Governor Stevenson would be a presidential candidate until the middle of July, which the Type D nominee, Stevenson—the compromise candidate, the reluctant candidate—had a tremendous amount of ground to make up in his race with the candidate who had been a forerunner for the Republican nomination since at least January, 1952.

The Type D or compromise convention may indicate that most of the important leaders of the party feel their party's chances in the presidential election are not particularly good. In 1952 only Senator Kefauver expended a significant amount of energy and organized a consistent and comprehensive primary campaign in order to win the nomination. Most of the other candidates, such as Senator Richard Russell of Georgia, Governor Adlai Stevenson of Illinois, and former Governor Averell Harriman of New York, expected that the presidential nomination would either be handed to them as compromise candidates or that they would win the presidency through the help of the various party leaders, but not with the support of the voters in primary elections.

One of the principal advantages of the Type D convention, which, in turn, can be a serious disadvantage in the Type C convention, is that the party is normally able to unify around the compromise candidate who is eventually selected. The Type C nominating convention is probably weakest in the sense that

frequently a large segment of the party is alienated by the convention proceedings. With one strong leader to push through a
platform and be nominated, there is ample room for discontent,
cries of foul play, and feelings of alienation from the general
convention process.

With a compromise candidate such dissatisfaction is less likely. As a matter of fact, lack of overwhelming delegate strength is
frequently one of the strongest points for the compromise candidate. Incapable of dominating the convention, he is forced to
cater to a number of different factions in order to acquire the
strength he needs to secure the nomination. Therefore, a Type
D convention is one in which a party is without a strong leader.
Because the party's probability of winning the presidency is
rather slight, the party's strongest leaders are not interested in
making an all-out effort to win the primaries and thus sew up
the convention nomination. The convention then turns to the
party bosses, who find a candidate who is acceptable to the
largest number of different factions, and this candidate becomes
the party's nominee.

The compromise nominee is generally the leader of a fairly
unified party, but a party that frequently lacks the vigor and
enthusiasm of a party that has gone through severe conflict in
the preconvention primary processes. The Type D nominee also
frequently lacks the charisma and publicity generally accorded
to a Type C, a Type A, or certainly to a Type B, nominee.

Adlai Stevenson was nominated in 1952 without entering any
primary contests or developing a significant nationwide organization with which to run a presidential contest. He was
then thrown into battle against General Eisenhower, who had
entered a number of preconvention primaries and who had a
nationwide organization already geared up and ready to go.
General Eisenhower came into the convention with several
primary victories under his belt. He was accorded widespread
publicity as a primary contender for the nomination; he won the
nomination by a bare majority; and he was forced then to
reconcile major differences between himself and the Taft forces.
As a matter of fact, in the campaign itself Eisenhower moved
significantly toward the Taft position on a number of important

issues, especially those concerning communism, corruption, and Korea. Eisenhower had a decisive advantage over Adlai Stevenson, who had built no national organization, attracted very little nationwide attention, and enjoyed only a smattering of preconvention support even among Democrats.

CHAPTER SEVEN

1900
McKinley vs. Bryan
TYPE B VS. TYPE C

The election of 1900 appears much more important in retro-spect than it did at that time. The second McKinley-versus-Bryan election marked a dramatic end to one segment of American politics and reinforced the onset of another segment, one that began in 1894 and continued for another thirty years. Between 1864 and 1896, the two major political parties, the Re-publican and the Democratic, were evenly matched. Even though the Democratic party won the presidency only twice, both times with Grover Cleveland, Democratic presidential candidates actually won a majority of the popular vote four times. In almost every presidential election the two major can-didates were within one or two percentage points of each other. In 1894 the Republicans seized control of Congress and held that control—except for an eight-year interlude between 1910 and 1918—until 1930.

The election of 1900 nailed the lid on the Democratic coffin for the next thirty years and established a new mode of electoral procedure. The election of 1900 also marked a dramatic change in the number of two-party states in which presidential can-didates had a reasonable opportunity to win electoral votes. The period from 1900 to 1930 was a period of one-party states. The election of 1900 marked the end of Negro voting as it had been practiced in the South since the end of the Civil War. Blacks were systematically being disenfranchised, and voters in general began to vote much less often than they had prior to 1900.

For an indication of this dramatically lowered voting percentage, we can look at the percentage of voters who voted before 1900 and the percentage of those who voted shortly afterwards. Between the years 1884 and 1896, approximately 61 percent of registered southern voters voted in presidential elections. Between 1904 and 1916, only 29 percent on the average voted. In the election of 1900, there were actually 377,000 fewer voters than there had been in 1896. Usually when the same two candidates face each other in two successive elections, the normal increase in the number of voters is diminished somewhat, that is, the normal 11 percent increase in voters is simply reduced to a lower percentage. Only rarely is there an actual drop in the total number of citizens voting from one election to the next, and certainly a drop of 377,000 voters is unusual. In the North, approximately 85 percent of the qualified voters voted for president between 1884 and 1896. By the time period 1904 to 1916 the percentage had dropped to 73. Between 1920 and 1932 only about 60 percent of the qualified northern voters were actually voting on election day.

By 1900, the Populists and the Democrats in the South had made their peace and had begun systematically to disenfranchise black voters. Thus began a thirty-year period in which, except for a significant break during the Woodrow Wilson era, the Republicans ruled the Northeast and Midwest and the Democrats controlled the South.

The Republican convention of 1900 was a Type B convention. The convention gave incumbent President McKinley 100 percent of the delegate votes on the first ballot. The four years from 1896 to 1900 had been reasonably successful years for the President. Considered by many to be an underrated president, McKinley had surrounded himself with first-rate intellects.

The McKinley campaign of 1900 is a good example of the tremendous strength of a Type B nomination. The Type B convention always has an incumbent running for renomination, and that incumbent is always supported by a unified party. The support of a unified party is frequently an indication that the preceding four years of the incumbent's administration have been fairly successful years. There have been none of the divisive intraparty squabbles that disturbed the administrations of

Chester Arthur and Benjamin Harrison. The party is generally satisfied with its incumbent, and usually when the party is satisfied with the incumbent, the country is, too.

There can be exceptions to this general rule, such as occurred in 1932, but generally when the incumbent president is supported by nearly 100 percent of his party's delegates at the nominating convention, it is a sign that the president's term of office has been fairly successful. Therefore, there is seldom a good reason to replace him with someone who has yet to be tested. The voters had a choice in 1900 of keeping a man, William McKinley, who had proven himself to be a successful administrator who had led the country through four sound and basically good years, or selecting a man, William Jennings Bryan, a Type C candidate, who had not yet proven himself as a nationally respected administrator.

A Type B convention, especially one in which an incumbent president receives 100 percent of the delegate votes on the first ballot, indicates that the party is strongly unified behind its candidate. Thus, the nominee goes into the presidential campaign with the backing of his entire party, a good record as an administrator, and the advantage of four years of nationwide exposure in the media. Under these conditions the Type B nominee is an extraordinarily difficult candidate to defeat.

When an incumbent president has been successful throughout his four years, it is likely that the opposition party will conduct either a Type C convention or a Type D convention. Either the party will have a titular leader, perhaps the man who lost against the incumbent president in the race four years earlier, or unable to decide on any one major leader for the nomination, the party will agree on a compromise candidate.

In 1900, a Type C candidate was chosen. There was no question in the minds of any of the delegates to the Kansas City, Missouri, convention that William Jennings Bryan would be the Democratic nominee for the presidency.

If there is one thing an opposition party should avoid at all costs, it is to have a nominating convention in which there is no significant competition for the presidential nomination. Lack of competition indicates two things: (1) only one man feels strongly that the incumbent party can be defeated in the November election; and (2) it will be difficult to generate enthusiasm because enthusiasm is normally a product of the conflict between candidates which precedes the convention.

Another problem a Type C candidate faces is related to the fact that approximately 11 percent more voters come into the electorate with each presidential contest. When a candidate is nominated for a second attempt at the presidential office, as William Jennings Bryan was in 1900, this 11 percent increase drops dramatically, which creates a serious disadvantage for the out-party. The out-party must attempt not only to substantially increase the proportion of new voters in the electorate but also to win a larger proportion of those new voters than the incumbent party. If the proportion of voters entering the electorate is not substantially increased, the chances of the out-party beating the incumbent are very slight.

In 1900, Bryan, whose nomination was uncontested, received 100 percent of the delegate votes on the first ballot. The only serious questions left for the convention to decide were those of a party platform and the selection of a vice-presidential candidate. No outstanding national leader, it seemed, wanted to be Bryan's vice-presidential nominee. Only one man, William Sulzer of New York, seemed to be very interested in the office. Sulzer was an active candidate, but his candidacy was laid to rest soon after Richard Croker sneeringly said, "Bryan and Sulzer! How long before everybody would be saying, 'Brandy and Seltzer'?" The nomination finally went to Adlai Stevenson, the 65-year-old former vice-president.

An incumbent president's renomination with 100 percent of the delegate votes on the first ballot, frequently indicates that his has been a very successful administration and that the party is satisfied with his four years in office. There are probably very few major factions opposing the renomination of the president because almost every faction in the party would have benefited to some extent from varying amounts of federal patronage.

On the other hand, when a challenger receives 100 percent of the delegate votes at his convention, it frequently means that either: (1) there are no serious challengers to the party's leader which may, in turn, be an indication of party weakness because individuals who might be serious challengers may feel that the president cannot be defeated easily, or (2) it may mean that the out-party did so poorly in the preceding congressional elections that there are few nationally known figures who would be in a position to compete for the party's nomination. It may also mean that the candidate received 100 percent of the delegate votes on the first ballot because it was generally accepted that he would be the party's nominee, and since he was not faced with formidable opposition, the other factions would rally around his candidacy, even though they might not be 100 percent in support of that candidacy.

In 1900, even though William Jennings Bryan won the Democratic presidential nomination on the first ballot, and even though there was no significant opposition to him, the Democratic convention itself came apart at the seams. Some of the eastern leaders of the party threatened to bolt because Bryan was determined to place the question of the free coinage of silver on the party's platform. "On July 1, 1900, five members of the Democratic national committee warned Bryan that if 16 to one was specifically reaffirmed [that is, the free coinage of silver] the East would be lost, the German and Scandinavian vote would go Republican and Democrats everywhere who were returning after their 1896 defection would leave once again." Bryan, though, believed that he was a national leader primarily because of his support among the silver people, and if he left the silver people in the lurch, he would lose his basic constituency and any real chance to win the presidency. Bryan felt that by holding the silver constituency he had only to add a half million to a million non-silver voters to win the presidency, whereas, if he cut the silver plank from the party's platform, he would have to struggle to find an entirely new constituency based on a new issue.

Most of the eastern Democratic leaders believed that because the government had remained on the gold standard and prosperity had been achieved between 1896 and 1900 without free silver, the issue of the free coinage of silver was dead. They also believed that any attempt to resurrect the free silver issue would lose votes. Bryan, of course, believed first and foremost in the free coinage of silver and stated that he would run only on a silver platform. The eastern delegates of the convention were willing simply to reaffirm the 1896 platform and omit any specific reference to free silver, but Bryan told the party leaders that he would run only if free silver were specifically endorsed in the party's platform. By a margin of one vote, the platform committee adopted the free silver plank that Bryan wanted, and Bryan accepted the party's nomination for the presidency.

The contest in the Democratic party over the question of the free coinage of silver in 1900 with all of the major party leaders from the eastern section of the country opposed to the resolution and Bryan the only national leader strongly in favor of it, shows how a Type C candidate can steamroller an obnoxious resolution through the convention, and how this resolution may, in turn, alienate large numbers of voters and factions of his own party.

The fact that Bryan was nominated by 100 percent of the delegates on the first ballot might seem to indicate that he was able to unite the party strongly behind him, but such was not the case. For various reasons, the delegates felt rather that it would be wiser to vote for Bryan than for any other candidate because no other major candidates were available. But, with this strength behind him, Bryan was able to ram through the convention a platform that appealed to him, but Bryan's determination to include the silver plank is a good example of how apparent strength in a Type C convention can actually be a severe weakness.

The 1900 Democratic convention had the appearance of unity but, in fact, Bryan had paid the political price of alienating several factions within his party merely to keep the silver forces together. If Bryan's nomination had been seriously contested by another candidate, and if Bryan had barely won the nomination with perhaps 50 to 55 percent of the delegate votes on the first ballot, the 1900 Democratic platform probably would not have contained a silver plank. Without the silver plank, it would have been easier to unify the party behind Bryan.

Other disputes divided the Democratic party in 1900, such as the issue of imperialism in the Philippines, but these other issues were hidden under the overriding question of the free coinage of silver. The Democrats were divided in 1900, but the Bryan forces were strong enough to keep these problems from being thoroughly aired in the convention and therefore were able to force the convention to accept whatever platform they felt was best. The feeling of unfairness that resulted among some delegates made it easier for factions of the party to withhold full support from Bryan in the general election.

CHAPTER EIGHT

1948
Truman vs. Dewey
TYPE B VS. TYPE D

By the spring of 1948, President Harry S. Truman was considered a sure loser in the 1948 presidential elections were he to obtain the Democratic nomination in his first attempt to win the presidency in his own right. Some nationwide polls showed Truman to have the support of as few as 36 percent of the nation's voters. Simultaneously, the Republican Congress, which had been elected in 1946 as the first Republican Congress since 1928, was devastating his legislative program.

Almost every faction of the Democratic party had some bone to pick with the Truman administration. The South was upset with Truman because of his progressive stances on civil rights legislation, and the liberals, many of whom were represented by the Americans for Democratic Action (ADA), were concerned because they thought Truman too conservative. Henry Wallace, who preceded Harry Truman as Franklin Roosevelt's vice-president, announced his intention of forming a Progressive party to counter the Truman policies, which Wallace believed were leading the United States inevitably into another world war.

The Democrats who believed that they could not win with Truman had to find someone who could replace him as the party's presidential nominee. The search for a candidate to replace President Truman quickly narrowed down to General Dwight D. Eisenhower. Because Eisenhower had already refused to be a candidate on the Republican ticket in 1948, many of the

Democrats believed that he might be willing to be drafted as a Democrat.

An extraordinary collection of politicians joined to support Dwight Eisenhower as the Democratic nominee for president. Finally, on July 9, just three days before the Democratic convention opened, Eisenhower cabled Senator Claude Pepper of Florida and stated, "No matter under what terms, conditions, or promises a proposal might be couched, I would refuse to accept the nomination." Perhaps in response to the Eisenhower refusal to accept a draft for the Democratic nomination and the realization that there was no one available to stop the nomination of the incumbent President, Senator Pepper announced on Sunday, July 11, that he himself would be willing to yield to a draft and become the Democratic candidate for the presidency. Two days later Senator Pepper withdrew his candidacy.

After an intensive battle over the civil rights plank, which saw the proposal of three southern minority planks, the Mississippi delegation and half of the Alabama delegation walked out of the convention; the remaining southerners threatened to leave later. On July 14, the convention chose Harry Truman as the Democratic nominee for the presidency. The southern delegates, in a last desperate effort to replace Truman with a candidate more acceptable to themselves and to reinforce the seriousness of their threatened bolt of the party, backed Senator Richard B. Russell of Georgia for the nomination. On the first ballot, President Truman received 923 ½ votes, Russell received 266, 18 ½ votes were scattered, and 23 ½ delegates did not vote.

Truman, therefore, received 78.3 percent of the delegate votes on the first ballot, which would place him in our Type B category, an incumbent president who receives more than 60 percent of the delegate votes on the first ballot. Seventy-eight percent delegate support does not place Truman in the ranks of incumbents who receive unanimous or nearly unanimous support from their parties, which would indicate a much higher level of support than Truman received.

Examples of candidates who received unanimous or nearly unanimous support from their party are incumbents Ulysses S.

Grant, who received the votes of 100 percent of the delegates supporting him on the first ballot in 1872, and President Grover Cleveland, who received 100 percent of the delegate votes on the first ballot in 1888. In 1900 William McKinley received 100 percent of the delegate votes on the first ballot. In 1904 Theodore Roosevelt received 100 percent. In 1916 Woodrow Wilson received 100 percent. In 1924 Calvin Coolidge received 96 percent of the delegate votes on the first ballot. In 1932 Herbert Hoover received 98 percent. In 1936 Franklin Roosevelt received 100 percent; in 1940, 86 percent, in 1944, 92.3 percent; and in 1964 President Lyndon Johnson received 100 percent of the delegate votes on the first ballot, as did President Eisenhower in 1956. President Truman, even though he did receive the backing of his party, did not receive it without some hesitation, which would tend to indicate that he would have been a less formidable candidate than an incumbent who received the unanimous backing of his party.

Even with the divided support he received from his party, Truman was still the incumbent president, and as such he was able to use the powers that accrue to an incumbent president seeking re-election.

The most serious weakness that can befall an incumbent president who is seeking his party's nomination for a second term stem from the problem of renomination by a divided party. A good example would be Benjamin Harrison in 1892 or William Howard Taft in 1912, both of whom were renominated by their parties with less than 60 percent of the delegate votes. A vote of less than 60 percent indicates to the electorate that there is less than solid support behind the incumbent. Such a delegate vote also may evidence severe dissatisfaction with the performance of the president in office.

Truman was able to avoid the serious splits that occurred in the Republican party in 1892 and in 1912, and he was able to unify the party behind himself, with the exception of the factions that broke off and formed the Dixiecrat party and the Progressives of Henry Wallace. Truman was almost the unanimous nominee of the Democratic party, except for the southern faction which supported Richard Russell. So Truman did have, except for the South and the Progressives, a united party behind his candidacy, a far different situation than that which faced the Republicans in 1892 and in 1912, when dissatisfaction with the incumbent was much broader and more intense.

The strength of a Type B candidate who has the unified support of his party lies in his ability to use the powers of the office of the presidency to his advantage in his presidential campaign. President Truman was an extraordinarily capable campaigner in this regard. He was able to use the power of the presidency in his political campaign as well as any candidate ever has before or since.

Soon after receiving his party's nomination, President Truman called a special congressional session to deal with the problems he had brought up earlier during the legislative session but which had been ignored by the Republican-controlled Congress. By calling this special congressional session, Truman was able to shift the voters' attention from his opponent and his own problems and failures as a chief executive to the Republican Congress. The Republican candidate, Dewey, was identified with the Republican congressional leaders, who were called the "do-nothings," and Dewey was forced to accept some of the criticism meted out to all Republicans because of their failure to enact legislation the president had proposed.

In effect, Truman ran against the Republican Congress instead of Thomas Dewey. He used such tactics as accusing the Republicans in farm areas of not providing grain storage bins and claiming that he was the only candidate who was sensitive to the problems of the farmers. Truman's action in calling a special session of Congress and his efforts to rivet attention on the problems of the Republican-controlled Congress at the expense of his opponent, Thomas Dewey, and his repeated identification of Dewey with an allegedly "do-nothing" Congress, exemplified some of the opportunities that can accrue to an incumbent who is running for re-election. Dewey could do nothing about the special session of Congress but hope that somehow the Republicans in Congress would get themselves and him out of a tricky situation.

The advantages of a compromise or Type D candidate, which

is what Thomas Dewey was in 1948, revolve around the fact that a compromise candidate can frequently unify a party that is split between several factions. The compromise candidate is often weakened by his lack of previous national exposure. Such a nominee may not be capable of infusing the party with the energy and vitality that characterize a party with a candidate who controls at least a majority of delegate votes on the first ballot.

Dewey was not saddled with the traditional weakness of the compromise candidate; he was well-known by the national electorate because he had been the Republican candidate for the presidency in 1944. But a serious obstacle was placed in his path by the historical tradition that Republicans did not renominate their titular leaders for the presidency. No Republican presidential nominee had ever been renominated for the presidency after suffering a defeat in the general election. Thus, even though Dewey was able to avoid one weakness of the compromise candidate, that is, the problem of lack of exposure, he was hampered by being a known quantity who was incapable of unifying and invigorating a party to the same extent that a true compromise candidate might have.

Dewey was opposed both in the primaries and in the convention by several strong candidates. Senator Taft of Ohio was again attempting to take a presidential nomination away from the liberal eastern establishment, which had controlled it since 1940. Harold Stassen, the Boy Wonder of Minnesota politics, conducted successful primary campaigns in several states before he was knocked out of the running with his stalemate in Ohio and his defeat in Oregon. Senator Arthur Vandenberg of Michigan was a last-minute candidate who hoped to gather enough votes to stop Dewey. Earl Warren, the governor of California, did little serious campaigning but hoped that he too would have a shot at the nomination as a compromise candidate.

On the first ballot, Dewey received 39.8 percent of the delegate votes. The only way to stop Dewey was for the Stassen forces and the Taft forces to unite behind either Taft or Senator Vandenberg. The crucial element in this potential stop-Dewey movement was Harold Stassen, who because of his defeat in Oregon was considered out of the running by most of the party's leading politicians. When Stassen refused to join forces with Taft and Vandenberg, Dewey was assured of the nomination. With the nomination went what was at that time considered to be almost certain election to the presidency of the United States.

The Republicans and their candidate Thomas Dewey did not completely understand the advantages possessed by an incumbent seeking renomination, and they also probably failed to understand the weaknesses inherent in the candidacy of a compromise candidate.

It is true that the incumbent president may have a difficult time generating vitality and momentum in his own campaign because he is usually considered the front-runner and has held the office long enough to allow people to become acquainted with him. In most cases, however, the resources of the incumbent are such that the enthusiasm of the general population is not necessary for re-election.

But the Type D or compromise candidate also has a difficult time injecting enthusiasm and vitality into his campaign. His selection as a compromise candidate when no candidate was able to gain a majority of the support of the party on the first ballot indicates that at least a majority, and in Dewey's case 61.2 percent of the Republican delegates on the first ballot, preferred someone other than Dewey for the presidency. When slightly more than 60 percent of the delegates prefer as their first choice someone other than a party's eventual nominee, it is difficult for the nominee to inject the same type of interest into his campaign that a candidate can when he is supported by at least a majority of the delegates on the first ballot. So while it often happens that both the Type B and the Type D candidate find it difficult to develop the type of enthusiasm that can be developed by a Type A candidate, the Type D candidate does not have the advantages of incumbency that the Type B candidate has.

The Republicans, then, had a candidate who had their unified support, but not their enthusiastic support. The Republicans should have kept in mind that the 11 percent average increase in the national electorate between presidential elections decreases, when a party renominates a defeated candidate for its leader. In renominating a defeated candidate, an out-party immediately falls behind the in-party because in most instances the out-party can use the momentum generated by a new leader to pick up a share of that 11 percent increase. The normal 11 percent increase drops somewhat when a defeated challenger is renominated because there is less excitement and enthusiasm about that candidate's nomination. The same thing that happened in 1948 happened again in 1956, except to a somewhat smaller degree.

Dewey was probably overly confident because the Democratic party appeared to be more split than it actually was, and because the incumbent president appeared to be more unpopular than he actually was. In turn, he compounded this misperception by believing his party to be more unified and more vigorous than it actually was. Dewey was seriously hurt by the loss of 74 Republican seats in Congress between 1946 and 1948. President Truman apparently was able to shift the blame for many of the nation's troubles to the Republican-controlled Congress, and thus identify Thomas Dewey with a body that was failing to cope with the nation's problems. In effect, the President removed the burden of responsibility from himself as the nation's chief executive and placed it on a group that had no effective spokesman to counter his advantages of publicity and initiative. Thomas Dewey, a Type D candidate, could not surmount these problems, and he was defeated by Type B candidate Harry Truman.

CHAPTER NINE

1928
Smith vs. Hoover
TYPE C VS. TYPE C

In 1928 both major political parties held steamroller conventions. Neither the Republican party nor the Democratic party had an incumbent who wished to be renominated for the presidency, and both of the major party nominees were nominated on the first ballot with more than 60 percent of the delegate votes. Herbert Hoover received 79.7 percent of the delegate votes on the first ballot to win the Republican nomination, and Al Smith, the governor of New York, received 77.4 percent of the delegate votes to win nomination on the first ballot at the Democratic nominating convention.

When both major parties have steamroller conventions, we would expect several things to happen. First, we would expect that both nominating conventions would be without serious discussion about either the major party nominees or the major party platforms. Second, we would not expect either candidate to have an advantage from his nomination inasmuch as both candidates were nominated at the same type of party convention and the conventions would tend to cancel each other out as influencing forces in the elections.

In order to predict the outcome of the 1928 election, instead of paying strict attention to the nominating conventions as indicators of party cohesion, party strength, and the attraction that each party has for the electorate, we would probably assume that the determining factors would be related to the comparative congressional strengths of the two parties during this period of time. Assuming that one party had been dominant before 1928 and assuming that the nominating conventions would cancel each other out as influencing forces, we would suggest that other forces would be at work during this period and that these other forces would be most influential in determining who would win the 1928 election.

During the eight years prior to the 1928 election, the Republican party controlled both the House of Representatives and the Senate. In the election of 1926, the Republicans won 42 more House seats than the Democrats. By 1928 the Republicans had increased their margin by an additional 30 seats. Clearly, the Republican party was the dominant party in the United States in 1928. It won 100 more congressional seats than the Democrats did. No presidential candidate whose party has lost more than 51 congressional seats has won the presidency since 1864. As a matter of fact, the largest number of House seats lost by the party of a presidential candidate who went on to win was the 51 seats lost by the Republicans to the Democrats in the 1968 general election.

If the assumption is made that conventions of the same type tend to cancel each other out as predictive mechanisms, it can be assumed that in 1928, with the Republican party obviously the dominant party in the country, the Republican nominee should have won the general election.

In every case in which both major parties have conventions of the same type, the party that wins the most congressional seats wins the presidency. In 1880, Garfield versus Hancock, Type D versus Type D candidates, the Republicans won 12 more House seats than the Democrats did, and James A. Garfield beat Winfield Scott Hancock by a mere 10,000 votes. In 1908, when both the major parties had Type C conventions, Republican William Howard Taft defeated Democrat William Jennings Bryan, and the Republicans won 47 more House seats than the Democrats. In 1920 both the Republicans and the Democrats had Type D nominating conventions. The Republicans nominated Warren G. Harding, and the Democrats chose James Cox. The Republicans won 170 more House seats than the Democrats, and Harding defeated Cox. And in 1928, when both the Republicans and the Democrats had Type C conventions, the Republicans won 100 more House seats than the Democrats, and Hoover easily defeated Smith.

Herbert Hoover decided early in 1928 that he wanted the Republican presidential nomination. He spent almost $400,000 in the primaries and was victorious in most of them. Hoover was opposed both by the Coolidge administration insiders and by most of the leaders of the Senate. But because no one could determine whether or not President Coolidge really wanted a second term on his own, and no one else could be coerced or convinced that they should make a serious effort to campaign against him, Hoover easily won the nomination on the first ballot. Apparently, President Coolidge was not interested in being renominated, so he stepped aside for Hoover. The administration insiders wanted to continue with President Coolidge; the Senate leaders wanted neither Hoover nor Coolidge, but they did not know who they could put up to provide the rallying point for an anti-Coolidge or anti-Hoover movement.

The Democratic convention in 1928 was not much more interesting than the Republican one. There was no stop-Al Smith movement, and no other strong candidates were put forward. Al Smith won on the first ballot and chose a southerner, Senator Joseph T. Robinson of Arkansas, as vice-president, the first residential southerner on a presidential ticket since the Civil War.

During the presidential campaign of 1928, the Republican party was basically united around its candidate, Herbert Hoover. There was some dissent in the farm states and Senator George Norris of Nebraska did defect, but these losses in the farm states by the Republicans were more than offset by the massive defections in the South from the Catholic Democratic candidate, Al Smith. Hoover's campaign was basically an above-the-battle stance in which he was portrayed as a great humanitarian, a great administrator, a great engineer, and the personification of the American business ideal. Hoover resisted the temptation to be enticed into a debate with the Democratic candidate, Al Smith, whose name he refused even to mention in public.

The Democratic candidate, Al Smith, who had been extraordinarily successful as governor of New York, was obviously running far behind from the beginning. The Democrats had suffered a disastrous defeat in 1924, receiving only 28.8 percent of the popular vote, actually receiving fewer popular votes than Woodrow Wilson had received eight years earlier in 1916. Smith had a considerable amount of ground to cover if he was going to bring the party back from 28.8 percent of the electorate to a majority in 1928. As it was, Smith's Catholicism alienated a number of southerners, even though he did have a south- ern vice-presidential candidate and did receive the support of some prominent southerners such as Senator Carter Glass of Virginia.

Hoover's strategy was to run a high-level statesman-like cam- paign in which Smith's name was not even mentioned. Smith, on the other hand, was running so far behind that he was forced to select a different strategy. He brought up all the issues, regardless of how popular they might be. In North and South Carolina, for example, Smith took a strong stand against the Republican-supported high tariffs and in favor of more im- migration from Europe.

On the religious issue, Smith used much the same argument that John Kennedy used a generation later. He argued that Catholics had the same right as any other religious minority to run for and hold national office. He argued for increased de- velopment of public power and was, in turn, called a socialist. He mentioned the Teapot Dome scandal and criticized the Coolidge administration for falling farm prices. Teapot Dome, though, was a forgotten issue, and discussing the problem of falling farm prices only reinforced the city-versus-country divi- sion to Hoover's advantage and Smith's disadvantage.

Smith did very well in the cities. He carried many large cities which had been traditionally Republican, such as New York, Cleveland, Boston, and St. Louis, and ran strongly in many others. The Democrats' success in the cities was a continuation of the movement begun in 1924 by the Progressives to break up the Republicans' urban power.

Smith lost because he was not capable of uniting the ur- ban groups that supported him with the rural forces that had been organized earlier by William Jennings Bryan. The urban strategy proved to be the proper strategy for the Democratic party of the future. The coming economic crisis (the depression) provided the final breakthrough for the Democratic party and decimated Republican strength throughout the cities. The depression also began to break down the old prejudices against governmental support of humanitarian, social, and economic projects. But it was to be Franklin Roosevelt rather than Al Smith who would rule that party of the future.

Smith's contribution to the emergence of the Democratic party as an urban-based party is generally acknowledged, but what is frequently forgotten is that Smith was almost single-handedly responsible for bringing the Democratic party back from its low point in 1924, when John W. Davis received 28.8 percent of the popular vote, to a position where it could capture the presidency just eight years later. In 1928, Smith received almost twice as many popular votes as Davis did in 1924.

As mentioned earlier, between 1896 and 1960 the electorate increased by about 11 percent between each presidential election year. In 1920, when the suffrage was extended to women, the percentage increase was much higher. In 1928 Al Smith was able to increase the Democratic percentage far above the 11 percent average. His vote total was 179 percent of that received by John W. Davis in 1924. Herbert Hoover received 136 percent the number of votes that Calvin Coolidge had received in 1924. Al Smith increased the Democratic percentage over the previous presidential election more than any other Democratic candidate between 1896 and 1960. Even Franklin Roosevelt in 1932 increased the Democratic party's percentage only to 152 percent of what it had received in 1928, approximately 27 percent less than the increase Al Smith was able to effect between 1924 and 1928. The only candidates who were able to increase their party's percentage of the vote more than Al Smith did in 1928 were Charles Evans Hughes in 1916, who increased the Republican party's proportion of the popular vote by about 245 percent (although it must be taken into account that this increase was based on the disastrous 1912 showing by William Howard Taft when the Republican party was split almost in two by the Progressive movement), and Warren G. Harding, who in 1920 increased the Republican percentage of the popular vote by 189 percent over 1916.

Al Smith actually ran a very effective campaign in 1928, and even though Herbert Hoover received almost 18 percent more of the vote—58.1 percent of the popular votes for Hoover compared with 40.8 percent for Smith—Smith's increased showing over 1924 was important in bringing the Democratic party back to a point where it could realistically be considered to have major party status and attraction.

It is interesting to consider what might have happened if the Democratic party in 1928, instead of having a Type C convention, had held a Type A convention in which there had been significant competition for the party's nomination. The disastrous defeat in 1924 and the party's only relatively good showing in 1926 made it very unlikely that many candidates would compete for the nomination in 1928. Even if nationally known figures had been available to compete for the 1928 Democratic nomination, they probably would not have expended their resources to achieve that nomination, because most astute political observers assumed in 1928 that the Republicans would win. Therefore, the circumstances surrounding the 1928 election make it difficult to imagine how a Type A convention could have occurred. Still, it is interesting to surmise what might have happened had the Democrats been able to conduct a Type A convention.

The increased competition for the party's nomination would have been evidence that significant numbers of party members felt that the party had a reasonable opportunity to win the presidency in 1928. Consequently, campaign contributions would doubtless have increased. Greater publicity for the competing Democrats would probably have added to the stature of the victor in the Democratic party's convention. As it was, with both Republican and Democratic nominees virtually unopposed, there was very little that either candidate, could do to prove his mettle to the voters in preconvention activities.

CHAPTER TEN

1868
Grant vs. Seymour
TYPE C VS. TYPE D

In 1868 Republicans tended to see their party as the natural repository of the nation's political power. The Republicans had led the country through the Civil War; they had provided a reconstruction program for the restoration of the Union. In general, they had guided the country through many of its darkest hours. In 1867 the appearance of a new coalition between the radical activists and the moderates seemed to indicate that the moderate reconstruction legislation of 1867 would not continue but that the election of a Republican in the fall of 1868 would be almost a certainty.

In one of the most peculiar political scenes since the turn of the century, the Republicans also found themselves at an advantage by having an unpopular Democrat as president at the same time that they controlled the federal administration. Andrew Johnson was a War Democrat from Tennessee, who joined Lincoln on the ticket of the Republican party in 1864 to symbolize a united determination on the part of both Republicans and Democrats to bring the Civil War to a successful conclusion. Thus, Abraham Lincoln, a Republican, had had Andrew Johnson, a Democrat, as his running mate in the 1864 presidential election.

When Lincoln was assassinated in 1865, Andrew Johnson became president of the United States. At that time the Republican party still controlled federal patronage and still supervised the organization of the former Confederate states who were being re-admitted to the Union. The Republicans were very careful to see that the newly elected officials from the defeated southern states and the newly emerging political organizations were supportive of the national programs and objectives of the Republican party.

The existence of an unpopular Democratic president, who had no control over the federal patronage system or the circumstances under which the southern states were being readmitted to the Union, created a very difficult situation for the Democrats. Here they were with an incumbent president they had not nominated and a federal bureaucracy and patronage system that were not under their control, even though the nominal head of that bureaucracy was a member of their own party.

The one advantage the Democrats appeared to have over the Republicans as the 1868 election year approached was the question of Negro suffrage, an issue that was a divisive factor among the Republicans and a unifying factor among the Democrats.

The Democrats attacked the Republicans for their support of Negro suffrage. They accused the Republicans of attempting to Africanize the South and argued that the Republicans were making an effort to impose Negro equality on the bulk of an unwilling nation. The accusations of the Democrats helped to divide the Republicans and unify the Democrats. The division within the Republican party was characterized by the extensive fights that took place over the Civil Rights Act of 1866 and the passage of the 14th Amendment to the Constitution.

Even though the Democratic party had an incumbent president, the party itself had been functionally out of power for the preceding eight years. They were unified on the question of Negro suffrage and considered themselves to be the only true national party. Interestingly, in the light of present-day public opinion on the different economic orientations of the two major parties, in 1868 the Democratic party considered itself to be the party of fiscal responsibility and the Republicans to be the party of reckless spending. The Democrats accused the Republicans of supporting an expanded and centralized government, and they argued that reconstruction programs and government in general could be more effective if they were decentralized.

General Ulysses S. Grant was nominated at the Republican convention in Chicago in the late spring of 1868, a Type C candidate. His unanimous nomination on the first ballot was accorded a tremendously enthusiastic reception.

The tenth Democratic national convention began on Independence Day in New York City. Only twice in the party's history were the Democrats to nominate truly reluctant candidates for president. 1868 was one of those two years. Horatio Seymour had been the governor of the state of New York at two widely separated times. He was elected governor of New York in 1852 but was defeated for re-election in 1854. In 1860, he had refused to be a candidate for the presidential nomination. He supported the Union cause when he was re-elected to the governorship in 1862. In 1864, he presided over the Democratic national convention but lost in his attempt to win re-election to the governorship during the same year. Almost all of the available records indicate that Horatio Seymour really had no desire to be the Democratic nominee for president in 1868. On the first ballot, he received no votes, and when he was finally nominated as a compromise candidate on the twenty-second ballot, he made a feeble attempt to refuse the nomination. He finally accepted it, however, and ran as a Type D candidate.

Whereas Grant's nomination was a forceful, unifying factor in the Republican party, Seymour's nomination had just the opposite effect on the Democrats. Apparently, even Seymour himself doubted that the Democratic National Committee would provide effective support for his candidacy. Seymour appeared to be one of those compromise candidates who are accepted by the convention because none of the front-runners has been able to win the nomination for himself. In the case of the Democratic national convention in 1868, the front-runners were Salmon P. Chase, George Pendleton, Andrew Johnson, and Thomas Hendricks. Each of these men, either by himself or with others, was able to prevent any of the remaining candidates from receiving the nomination.

Much of the blame for this inability of the Democrats to nominate their strongest candidate must lie with the two-thirds rule that governed the party's voting procedures until 1936. The two-thirds rule stated that the Democratic nominee for the presidency had to receive the support of two-thirds of the convention's delegates in order to receive the party's nomination; this meant that any candidate who could control one-third plus one of the convention delegate votes could stop the nomination of any other candidate. Many of the strongest candidates between 1864 and 1932 were men who had created enough animosity among strong opponents during their public careers to make it fairly easy to obtain the one-third plus one of the votes necessary to prevent their nomination.

The difficulties that Horatio Seymour brought to the Democratic campaign of 1868 help explain why a party that nominates a relatively weak compromise candidate is in serious trouble when it is competing with a universally accepted candidate, such as Ulysses S. Grant.

Not all compromise candidates are as weak as Horatio Seymour was in 1868, but a compromise candidate can be a serious liability for a party when it is competing against an opposition headed by a strong leader and a well-liked and widely accepted nominee. Horatio Seymour was a nominee that most factions of the Democratic party in 1868 could accept, but he was not one who could rally the party around him and lead it in the vigorous campaign that would be needed to defeat a candidate of Grant's popularity and national stature.

Seymour's record in itself was not outstanding. He had consistently run behind the party's ticket in his gubernatorial races and, in fact, had been defeated three out of the five times that he joined the race for governor of New York. Seymour had never held national office and his career was associated entirely with the state of New York. He was also handicapped by the fact that it was widely believed he had been sympathetic to the Copperheads in the New York draft riots of 1863. Seymour was nominated, nonetheless, because none of the other stronger candidates was able to overcome the one-third plus one veto held by the remaining active candidates.

The Democrats should have been able to use the issue of Negro suffrage to their advantage in 1868 to split the Republicans. Instead they were divided themselves over the presidential and vice-presidential nominees because of the dampening lack of enthusiasm that followed the nomination of Seymour. But the attempts to replace Seymour on the ballot with someone else never gathered momentum, and the ticket remained Horatio Seymour for president and Frank Blair for vice-president, and Grant was elected with 52.7 percent of the popular vote.

The campaign and election of 1868 provide good examples of one of the strengths of a Type C candidate and the serious weaknesses that may accompany the nomination of a Type D candidate. In the case of Ulysses S. Grant, the Republican convention of 1868 was a strong C convention. At this convention there was no incumbent president seeking the nomination, although the Republicans had maintained control of the federal bureaucracy and federal patronage through the re-election of their nominee, Abraham Lincoln, in 1864. But, because Lincoln had selected a Democrat as his vice-presidential nominee, the Democratic party was stuck with the unpopular Andrew Johnson while the Republican position was bolstered both by control over the federal patronage and supervision of the re-entrance of the southern states into the Union.

Before the conventions of 1868, there had been indications that the Republican party might be divided over the issue of Negro suffrage, while the Democrats appeared to be strongly united on the question. But at their convention in late May of 1868 the Republicans were strongly united behind one candidate, General Ulysses S. Grant. Grant had the support of 100 percent of the delegates on the convention's first ballot, and no significant factions opposed his nomination.

The tremendous support for General Grant assured the Republicans of a strong, nationally known candidate to lead the party's ticket. By emphasizing the role of their candidate and de-emphasizing the importance of the substantive issues in the campaign, the Republicans were able to generate unified support for General Grant. The universal support given to a powerful candidate is one of the strongest forces activated by a Type C convention. The depth and breadth of support that the 1868 Republican convention gave Grant fostered a level of vitality and a spirit of unity that simply could not be duplicated by the Democratic convention, which was left with a compromise candidate who had received no votes at all on the first ballot.

Grant was so popular that his candidacy alone was able to unite various factions of the party which were not in complete agreement on the question of their own candidate's abilities, and the major issues in the campaign proceeded to divide the Democrats as much as they did the Republicans.

The Republicans had nominated a popular candidate and were well organized and well financed. Their Type C convention had unanimously nominated on the first ballot a candidate who enjoyed the popular support of every faction of his party. Grant probably could have been defeated by a powerful, unified, and well-financed organization. But the Democrats, already divided over the greenback question, were forced to select a compromise candidate for president who not only was unable to unify the party around his candidacy but also did much to divide the party further.

A Type D convention has a potential advantage in that a compromise candidate can bring unity when the convention is deeply divided. But the nomination of Seymour, in addition to incorporating the normal weaknesses of a Type D candidate, failed to provide the advantage of unifying the party around a candidate who at least would not be anathema to large factions within the party. It was not that Seymour was so obnoxious to members of his party; it was just that he was considered to be a weak candidate who was likely to lose. Thus, the Democrats' Type D convention produced a compromise candidate who was incapable of unifying and leading their party and unable to inject the Democratic campaign with the vitality and organization necessary to defeat the Republican nominee.

1892
Cleveland vs. Harrison
TYPE C VS. TYPE E

Four years prior to the 1892 election, the Republican party had won the presidency because of the extraordinary unity with which the party supported its presidential candidate, Benjamin Harrison. In 1888, Benjamin Harrison had been a Type D candidate, and one who exhibited some of the best qualities that typify a candidate from a Type D convention. One of the most powerful forces that can be unleashed with a Type D convention is that of the unity a candidate can create when he is able to bring warring factions of a party together and, in the process, infuse the party with a cohesiveness that one of the party's stronger candidates could not achieve. Harrison was able to unify the Republicans in 1888, and even though he received fewer votes than the incumbent President Grover Cleveland, he won the presidency.

By 1892, Harrison had alienated many of the most powerful bosses in the Republican party. Matthew Quay of Pennsylvania, Thomas C. Platt of New York, and Thomas B. Reed of Maine had all become disenchanted with Benjamin Harrison as president of the United States, because of Harrison's refusal to provide the federal patronage that would have strengthened these local party bosses. The disaffection of these party bosses was a significant factor in weakening the party unity that had carried Harrison to victory in 1888.

In addition to the party unity shown in 1888, the Republicans, who had lost the presidency in 1884 for the first time since 1856, had exhibited a sense of crisis and a sense of dedication

that carried them on to victory. By 1890, the feeling of dedication had disappeared, and the Democrats overwhelmed the
Republicans in the congressional elections. The Democrats won
231 House seats to only 88 for the Republicans.

The specter of probable defeat shadowed the Republicans'
prospects in 1892. Harrison had won the presidency in 1888 as a
compromise candidate because his party had closed ranks
behind him in its drive to recover the presidency it had lost for
the first time in twenty-four years in 1884. Although he had
received fewer popular votes than his opponent, he had won
because he was able to carry several critical industrial states on
the issues of tariff protection and internal development. By
nature a cold, aloof man, Harrison alienated many members of
his own party. He knew prior to the nominating convention of
1892 that he would probably receive the nomination but realized that there would be considerable dissatisfaction with his
nomination. He also realized that his nomination would probably be difficult to accept for many Republicans who would have
preferred that someone else be the party's presidential nominee.

The Republican convention did renominate Benjamin Harrison on the first ballot despite considerable support for James G.
Blaine of Maine and William McKinley of Ohio. Blaine had
been the Republican nominee in 1884 when the party lost the
presidency for the first time since 1860, and William McKinley
was to be the party's nominee in 1896. In 1892, Harrison received 58.6 percent of the Republican delegate votes on the first
ballot and thus was a Type E candidate.

The apparent lack of support for the incumbent president
made it clear that some Republican leaders were indifferent, and
others were probably even hostile, to Harrison's nomination. In
renominating an incumbent with only 58.6 percent of the delegate votes on the first ballot, the Republican party was showing
little of the fighting spirit and the sense of urgency that had
carried it to victory in 1888.

The Republicans in 1892 demonstrated why a Type E candidate is so likely to lose the presidency. A Type E convention is
a convention that renominates an incumbent president for a second term but nominates him with less than 60 percent of the

votes on the first ballot. A vote of less than 60 percent for an incumbent president is a clear sign that major factions of the party are dissatisfied with his administration and his performance in office.

If party leaders are ambivalent with regard to an incumbent president, they are not likely to perform their roles in the campaign with the zeal and dedication that are crucial if the party is to win re-election. If large factions of the party feel dissatisfied with the incumbent's leadership during the past four years, it is difficult to see how they can be motivated to work hard for four more years of that leadership. In fact, in situations in which the incumbent does not command unified support, some segments of the incumbent's own party probably would prefer that the incumbent lose. The insurgents would then have an opportunity to find another candidate for the presidential battle four years later. If the incumbent wins without the support of large factions of his party, he is obviously stronger than those factions and able to perform adequately without their help. Party insurgents would probably find themselves in a more advantageous position, therefore, if the incumbent they did not support at the convention were to lose the election.

The Type E candidate has the severe disadvantage of having performed for four years in office to the dissatisfaction of party members who, ideally, would have been satisfied. If neither the party bosses nor the rank and file of the party are satisfied with his performance in office, the incumbent chief executive has probably failed to satisfy the great masses of the electorate as well. The rank and file of the party are not likely to support such a candidate with much enthusiasm. Thus, the Type E nominee is in an extraordinarily weak position; he enjoys the unqualified support of neither the party leaders, the party rank and file, nor, in all probability, the vast majority of the American electorate. A feeling of resignation usually pervades the ranks of the party and its leaders, instead of the dedication and determination necessary if the incumbent is to win the election.

In contrast to the tepid tone of the Republican convention, in which an incumbent president had been nominated by little more than a majority of the delegates on the first ballot, were

the more spirited proceedings at the Democratic convention as
the party rallied around its presidential candidate of 1884 and
1888, former President Grover Cleveland. This is not to suggest
though, that the Democratic convention was an especially unified and happy one. Cleveland came into the Democratic convention in the lead, and even though some groups supported
New York Governor David Hill and Arthur Pue Gorman, U.S.
Senate minority leader from Maryland, Cleveland was generally
accepted as the man most likely to receive the Democratic
nomination. Gorman, for example, refused to oppose Cleveland
because he believed that Cleveland would receive the nomination and that divisions within the party would ruin the party's
chances of defeating the incumbent Harrison.

A major split occurred within the Democratic party when the
platform committee refused to accept the western demand for a
plank supporting the free coinage of silver. Some of the embittered western and southern Democrats then threatened to
bolt the party, following the lead of the 1890 Populist movement, which had captured nine congressional seats. As over-
production in wheat, corn, and cotton pushed commodity
prices down, the farmers of the Midwest and the South began to
talk of a third-party movement. The refusal of the Democrats in
1892 to accept the silver plank simply accelerated the movement
to break away from the Democrats and start a party.

The break by the free silver people is an example of the fac-
tionalization that can occur at a Type C convention. Grover
Cleveland received 67.9 percent of the delegate votes on the first
ballot, and with this support the convention became very much
a Grover Cleveland convention. The convention was a classical
Type C convention. The nominee, unlike Ulysses S. Grant, who
had the unanimous support of the convention, did not have the
unanimous support of his party but he was strong enough to
avoid having to make major concessions to factions dissatisfied
with his candidacy or with his platform. Such dissatisfied factions feel that they have been effectively shut out by the party.
Because they feel they have not had a fair hearing in the convention and the convention has turned overwhelmingly to a

stronger leader whom they do not like, such groups may feel they have little choice but to bolt the party. And bolt the party is exactly what some of the western and southern factions threatened to do over the silver question and over some elements of the proposed Populist program.

Both the Type C and the Type E conventions may suggest serious difficulties. The Type C convention, unless its candidate receives the type of support that was received by Ulysses S. Grant in 1868, may produce a candidate who receives the overwhelming support of the majority of the convention delegates, and yet is not fully acceptable to all segments of the party. The candidate's overwhelming acceptance makes it unnecessary for him to offer compromises to the disaffected elements within the party, and, shut out and silenced, these disaffected elements may either threaten a walk-out or, in fact, bolt the party.

The Type E convention on the other hand is even weaker than the Type C convention. Whereas the Type C convention may lose the support of one or two factions within the party, the Type E convention itself signifies the dissatisfaction of large segments of the party with the performance of its incumbent in office. If, after having the opportunity to receive patronage from their incumbent and seeing how effectively he has performed the duties of chief executive, many segments of the party are still unwilling to support him for a second nomination, the disappointment with his performance must be deep. Severe dissatisfaction with the incumbent plus what is frequently the incumbent party's lack of a sense of the crisis and urgency that can pervade the out-party, further weaken the ability of the Type E nominee to rally his party around his candidacy and lead it to victory in a presidential election.

Neither Cleveland nor Harrison excited the voters. One observer of the election of 1892 was supposed to have suggested that "each side would have been glad to defeat the other, if it could have done so without electing its own candidate." Neither Harrison nor Cleveland was able to dramatically unify his party, but, as was mentioned earlier, the candidate of the Type C convention, Cleveland, is somewhat better off than that of the

Type E convention, Harrison. And in 1892 the Democrats were slightly more unified than the Republicans and slightly less dissatisfied with their candidate, who had not spent the preceding four years in office.

CHAPTER TWELVE

1880
Garfield vs. Hancock
TYPE D VS. TYPE D

The Republican and Democratic party nominating conventions of 1880 were marked by some of the most vicious intraparty squabbling ever seen. Both parties witnessed intense infighting over the presidential nomination, the party platform, and the division of the anticipated spoils. Interestingly, the differences between the candidates and between the parties themselves in 1880 were minimal. Perhaps the lack of major differences between candidates or between the parties heightened the intraparty battles that took place over the disposition of the expected governmental rewards.

On the issues of tariff, silver coinage, and the admission of Chinese immigrants to the United States, it was very difficult to distinguish between the two parties. Since Rutherford B. Hayes had removed the last of the Union troops from the South in 1877, the question of reconstruction was no longer a major issue. Between 1876 and 1880 there had been relative prosperity, and both farmers and laborers were quiescent during the period immediately preceding the conventions.

The Type D convention, the compromise convention in which there is no incumbent and no candidate receives more than 50 percent of the vote on the first ballot, usually indicates that the party has no strong leader: for various reasons strong national leaders within the party have been unable to round up at least a majority of the support of the party's delegates. The party seen in the Type D convention is split into numerous factions, none of which is able to bring together a majority of the convention delegates to secure the nomination for their candidate. The convention then may be marred by severe infighting in the search for a candidate who will provide the unity that none of the major factions' candidates can. Usually in a Type D convention the party turns to a compromise candidate who is not a strong, well-known figure in the party. The compromise candidate is selected usually because a strong figure would have been nominated on an earlier ballot or else he would have unified his opposition enough for them to prevent his receiving the nomination on any ballot.

In terms of the availability of strong leaders in 1880, the Republicans were in a much more favorable situation than the Democrats. The Republicans, after all, still had as a possible candidate their former two-term President, Ulysses S. Grant. Grant had recently returned from a triumphant around-the-world trip, during which he was received abroad as America's answer to European royalty. Arriving home from his world tour, Grant received the adulation of hundreds of thousands of admirers, who gave the impression that Grant could easily be elected as America's first president to serve more than two terms. Grant, who was not independently wealthy and had no skills but those of the military, had enjoyed the style of life to which he had become accustomed as a resident of the White House; he found the prospect of serving a third term as president very attractive.

Several of the Republican leaders, including John Logan of Illinois, J. Donald Cameron of Pennsylvania, and Roscoe Conkling of New York, strongly supported Grant's effort to gain a third nomination. Despite the scandals that had occurred during Grant's eight years in office, these Republican leaders believed that the tremendous popular reception accorded Grant on his return from his European trip would guarantee victory for the Republicans in November and thus assure them of another four years of patronage.

The opposition to electing a president to serve three terms was probably much more widespread and severe than the Grant supporters at first believed. Many of the delegates who believed that a third term was not a wise move, but who still were longing for a strong, popular leader, looked to James G. Blaine of Maine. Blaine and Grant together controlled almost two-thirds of the convention delegates. But neither could get the nomination without the support of the other. Because each was determined that if he could not have the nomination, neither could the other, the nomination was destined to go to a compromise candidate, someone who was not a favorite at the beginning of the convention.

On the thirty-sixth ballot at the convention, with Grant and Blaine hopelessly deadlocked, it became apparent that some other candidate would have to be advanced to receive the nomination. The man to whom the convention turned on the thirty-sixth ballot was James Garfield, a congressman from Ohio. Garfield was a candidate without the national renown of Blaine or Grant, but he was able to contribute considerable unity to the Republican party in 1880. And after one of the most biting and vicious conventions ever held, the Republicans needed a candidate of Garfield's unifying capabilities to lead them in the campaign ahead. *The Nation* magazine, which opposed both Grant and Blaine, said that "the result has almost the air of a special providence."

It was intriguing that a party so unified on issues could be so severely split by personalities. The fight at the convention was never over which issues the party should support in its platform, but rather over which faction of the party should divide the spoils when the presidency was won. The Stalwarts, who were the Conkling and Grant men, fought the Half-Breeds, who were the Blaine men, over credentials and over methods of voting. The convention proceedings became almost ludicrous at times. Any suggestion forwarded by one faction was almost certain to be opposed by the other faction, simply because the opposition had suggested it. The questions at stake, although critical, were questions to decide which local Republican leaders were to receive the greatest benefits if a Republican candidate for the presidency were to win.

Although Garfield was successful in bringing unity to the Republican party in 1880, that unity was not immediately forthcoming. The Conkling and Grant forces were bitterly op-

posed to the nomination of Garfield at first, and by the time the
convention ended the party was severely split between the
Stalwarts and the Half-Breeds. Chester A. Arthur was selected
as the party's vice-presidential nominee because he was considered a major cog in the Conkling machine in New York City.
Arthur, who had earlier been removed as the New York collector of customs during a reform investigation, was offered the
vice-presidential nomination in an attempt to bring the Conkling forces back into the party. Roscoe Conkling tried to talk
Arthur out of the vice presidency, but Arthur, claiming that it
was higher than any honor he ever expected to attain in his
lifetime, said that he had no intention of refusing it. Eventually,
though, the Conkling men, perhaps because Garfield supposed-
ly offered them substantial spoils, returned to the party fold
and thereafter provided considerable support for the Garfield
victory.

The Democrats had not won the presidency for almost twen-
ty-five years by the time the 1880 convention rolled around. As
a result of this long absence from the center of national power,
the Democratic leadership tended to be locally rather than nationally concentrated. The strength of the Democratic party was
based in state and local politics. The Democrats who had been
able to survive, politically and economically, were those who
had been able to build up powerful local machines and use
whatever local and state patronage was available to keep them
running. The local orientation of the party leaders made it
somewhat more difficult for the Democrats to develop nationally oriented candidates than it was for the Republicans, who had
controlled the federal administration since 1860.

At the 1880 convention, the Democratic party was somewhat
more split on the issues than the Republicans. There were hard
money-soft money differences, there were conflicting opinions
about the tariff, and there was a critical split between Tammany
Hall and the 1876 presidential nominee Samuel J. Tilden. In
view of these rifts in the party, it was imperative that the
Democratic convention find a candidate who could bring the
warring factions together in an atmosphere of compromise.
Ideally, a candidate who had very few enemies was preferable to

one who was so strong that he might alienate one of the major factions in the party. General Winfield Scott Hancock was a compromise candidate of whom almost no one disapproved, and about whom few people had much to say, bad or good. He appeared to be the perfect candidate for the year in which the Democrats were desperately searching for unity and a compromise candidate.

Hancock could unite the Democratic party, but the qualities that made him so attractive as a unity candidate also made him a relatively poor campaigner. He was capable of unifying the party, but his lack of strength and his inability to generate much enthusiasm among the rank and file made it difficult for the Democrats to expect to carry the day. Hancock received just over 40 percent of the delegate votes on the first ballot, but the convention stampeded to him after the second ballot. Hancock was not a particularly attractive candidate, but he was an important compromise candidate in a situation where the Democrats were not blessed with any heavy favorites or popular leaders.

Because both parties held the same type of convention in 1880, our formula suggests that we should look elsewhere to understand the influence of various forces on the outcome of the presidential election. In a campaign year in which both conventions were Type D, we would anticipate two compromise candidates, neither of whom would exhibit the leadership or the drive that we might expect from Type A, B, or C candidates. We would expect that the outcome of the election would be decided by variables other than those associated with the national party conventions. The outcome of the 1878 congressional elections indicated that the presidential contest in 1880 would probably be very close if neither candidate was nominated in a convention that indicated that he should be favored. In 1878 the Democrats held a slight advantage in the House of Representatives, 149 seats to 130 for the Republicans. In the 1880 election the contest for control of Congress was almost as close as the contest for the presidency, with the Republicans holding a 12-seat advantage, 147 to 135.

It was generally believed in 1880 that whoever was able to

carry New York State would almost undoubtedly win the presidency. With both parties split in New York, it was not clear at the beginning of the campaign which party would be favored as the more unified. Because Chester Arthur was on the ticket and because Garfield was able to soothe the ruffled feelings of Roscoe Conkling, the Republicans were able to overcome more of their differences than the Democrats. Apparently, the patronage that Garfield offered Conkling also had something to do with Conkling's efforts to unite the New York party and win the 1880 presidential election.

The New York Democratic party was split between the two Democratic leaders, John Kelly of Tammany Hall and Samuel Tilden, the party's nominee in 1876. In the 1880 mayoralty contest in New York City, John Kelly supported a Catholic to be New York's first non-Protestant mayor in two hundred years. Kelly's support of a Catholic split the Democrats and made it difficult for Hancock to gain the large majorities in New York City needed to offset the expected Republican victory in upstate New York. New York was the crucial state, and James Garfield was able to carry it, primarily because of the support of Roscoe Conkling and his Republican organization and because of the split between John Kelly of Tammany Hall and Samuel Tilden.

Apparently, John Kelly was not particularly concerned at Hancock's failure to carry New York State. A Democratic president might be more of a threat than a support to him. After twenty years out of national office, many local Democratic bosses perceived a Democratic president as a potential competitor for patronage. By helping to elect a Democrat to the presidency, the local leaders might be elevating a man who would be capable of undercutting their own personal power bases.

Garfield won the presidency 4,454,416 votes to 4,444,952 votes for Hancock, that is, by a margin of about 10,000 votes. Only the South went solidly for Hancock, a clear indication that the solid Democratic South was rapidly becoming a reality and an asset that the Democrats could not ignore in the future.

Both parties nominated compromise candidates in the absence of strong leaders who had unified party support. Although both compromise candidates worked to draw the factions in their parties together, the Republicans' efforts were more successful than those of the Democrats.

CHAPTER THIRTEEN

1912
Wilson vs. Taft
TYPE D VS. TYPE E

By all rights, William Howard Taft probably should have been renominated easily for president in 1912. Since Chester Arthur in 1884 no Republican president had ever been refused renomination. The Republican party at the federal level had been victorious at the polls consistently until 1910, when, for the first time since 1892, the Democrats gained control of the House of Representatives. Between 1908 and 1910 the Democrats picked up 56 House seats.

As president, Taft had been surprisingly progressive. He had dissolved more trusts and presided over the granting of more acreage to the national parks and forest reserves in three years than Theodore Roosevelt had in seven. Taft was also responsible for enacting more social legislation than Theodore Roosevelt, even though Roosevelt had been chief executive more than twice as long as Taft.

In 1912 the nation was generally prosperous; prices for farm goods were relatively high, and the stock market was on the rise. The only problems on the horizon were the increasing cost of living and the tension that was created by impending conflict with Mexico.

Notwithstanding apparent national prosperity and the four years of peace over which President Taft had presided, two formidable challengers stood in the way of his renomination to the presidency. Senator Robert M. LaFollette of Wisconsin was the senatorial leader of the Progressive movement, which was demanding that the nation's government be more sensitive to the needs and demands of the people. The Progressives proposed changes in political procedure that would improve the capabilities of the nation's voters to effect legislative programs that affected their lives. The Progressives demanded innovations such as the recall of judges, the direct election of senators, the initiative, the referendum, and the income tax as part of their attempt to make the government more democratic. They believed that voters should have the right to elect the nation's leading public officials and to remove them from office if they proved unsatisfactory. They also believed that citizens should have the right to initiate legislation on their own behalf if their elected representatives failed to do so.

The Progressives generally believed that the government, as it existed in 1912, was primarily concerned with benefiting the well educated. By instituting such reforms as the recall of judges, the direct election of senators, the initiative, the referendum, and the income tax, the Progressives were hoping to force the government to be more responsive and sympathetic to the demands and the needs of all American voters.

The intellectual impetus for much of the Progressive movement was to be found in Herbert Croly's book, *The Promise of American Life.* One of Croly's primary arguments was that the proposed structural changes in the American government would not in themselves significantly alter the distribution of the nation's power or wealth, but by altering the form of the government, the substance, that is, the distribution of power and wealth, could in the long run be modified. It was argued that, rather than taking significant amounts of wealth from the rich and diverting it to the poor, the government should increase its control of corporations and be more concerned with the protection of the nation's workers. Croly felt that the government should attempt to provide an atmosphere relatively free of legal entanglements in which labor unions could function, and that it should provide a protective umbrella under which wage earners, small businessmen, consumers, and investors could be protected from the greedy and unscrupulous. It was argued that only the government had enough power to produce the types of substantive changes that were necessary to maximize the promise of democracy for every man, woman, and child in America.

Once Theodore Roosevelt returned from his African safaris and charged into the leadership of the Progressive forces, the national chances of Senator LaFollette were effectively extinguished. Theodore Roosevelt provided a dramatic focal point around which the anti-Taft forces could rally. But it was neither the Progressives nor the leadership of LaFollette and Roosevelt alone which split the Republican party so disastrously.

By 1912, a split in the Republican party between the traditional Republican forces and the Progressives seemed inevitable. The political gyrations the Republican party was forced to go through in order to keep itself together made it functionally incapable of providing the unity of direction and cohesion a majority party needed in order to maintain its control of the country's political machinery. The Republican party had long been committed to rather conservative policies; at the same time, it was depending for electoral support upon the rapidly urbanizing East and the increasingly agrarian West. In both sections, the spirit of insurgency had grown intense.

Roosevelt's ostentatious trustbusting, his frequent moralizing, and his attempts to regulate the railroad industry gained him significant support among some of the traditional Populist elements. By avoiding many of the radical overtones that frequently characterized Populist rhetoric, Roosevelt managed to expand the strength of the Republicans considerably in many of the western agrarian areas. By arguing that the consumer needed to be protected by the federal government, that labor should be given greater freedom within which to organize, and that the government should intervene on behalf of the rights of women and children, Roosevelt was able to contribute to the increasing dissatisfaction of eastern Republicans with their party. Roosevelt attempted to point out that the Republican doctrines in 1912 were not as responsive as the Progressive arguments were, and that, in many cases, they were as archaic and unresponsive to the needs of the rapidly urbanizing areas of the East as the narrow, agrarian-oriented doctrines espoused by William Jennings Bryan had been in 1896, 1900, and 1908.

Herbert Croly's book, *The Promise of American Life,* was published in 1909. In 1910, the spirit of progressivism had begun to build, a spirit that took political form in the 1910 attempts to limit the dictatorial powers of House Speaker Joe Cannon and in the conflict over the Payne-Aldrich tariff legislation and the Mann-Elkins Act, which attempted to increase the regulation of interstate carriers.

By 1910, President Taft was beginning to see the handwriting on the wall regarding the danger to the Republican party posed by its increasingly belligerent Progressive element. Taft attempted to purge the Republican Progressive insurgents in 1910, and contributed to the considerable Democratic victories in the congressional elections in the process. Taft's attempt to purge the Progressives from the Republican party served only to turn the leadership of the House of Representatives over to the Democrats and to solidify the Progressive opposition, which now included Senators LaFollette, Dolliver, Cummins, Beveridge, Clapp, and Borah.

In his Osawatomie, Kansas, speech on the "new nationalism," Theodore Roosevelt moved to the point where a split with the regular Republican party became almost inevitable. In this speech, Roosevelt argued forcefully that property rights must be held secondary to human rights, and he suggested a number of reforms, which included taxing the wealthy to benefit the poor, and increasing federal regulation of corporations and, at the same time, reducing the rights of individual states vis-à-vis the federal government.

In 1910, the Democrats had elected their first New England senator since the Civil War and gained three New England state houses for Democratic governors, and it had become obvious that the Democratic party was no longer the fossilized relic it had seemed to be since 1896. The electoral successes of the New England Democrats also provided fuel for an anticipated struggle for the 1912 Democratic nomination and plainly signified that the strength of the Democrats was rising while the Republicans were weakening as a result of the well-publicized split between the Progressive and Traditional wings of their party.

Theodore Roosevelt, who had already served seven years as president of the United States, publicly opposed William Howard Taft when he decided to try for the Republican nomination. Frequent personal attacks by the two candidates characterized the presidential primaries. So bitter was the barrage of personal criticism between the candidates that the issues in the primaries were frequently obscured.

The direct primary was used extensively for the first time in 1912. In the primaries, Roosevelt won almost 400,000 more votes than President Taft. Roosevelt won 1,157,397 votes, Taft 761,716, and Senator LaFollette 351,043. Roosevelt won primaries in Pennsylvania, California, Minnesota, Nebraska, Maryland, South Dakota, Ohio, and New Jersey. Taft, meanwhile, was concentrating most of his efforts in the states that did not hold direct primaries.

By concentrating his efforts in the nonprimary states, Taft was able to win the Republican nomination with 52 percent of the delegate votes on the first ballot, the lowest percentage an incumbent president had ever received in being renominated. The only other renominated president since 1864 who received less than 60 percent of the vote on the first ballot was Benjamin Harrison, who received 58.6 percent in 1892; this, of course, does not take into consideration the efforts of Andrew Johnson in 1872 and Chester Arthur in 1884, neither of whom received their party's nomination. The platform that went with Taft's nomination was basically conservative, but one with several progressive features. The platform proposed some legislative protection for women and children laborers and supported a workmen's compensation program.

When Roosevelt bolted from the Republican party and formed the new Bull Moose or Progressive party, the Democratic party found itself in a serious quandary. The new Bull Moose party was to the Democratic party approximately what the Liberal Republican party had been to the Democratic party in 1872, when it nominated Horace Greeley. With the Conservative Taft nominated by the Republicans, and the Progressive Roosevelt nominated by the Bull Moose party, the Democrats knew that nominating a Conservative Democrat could very well give the presidency to Theodore Roosevelt. They had little fear that Taft would win the election, but were concerned at the likelihood of a split in the minority of Conservative votes between Taft and a Conservative Democratic nominee.

Many of the Democratic Progressives turned to Speaker of the House Champ Clark as the most likely candidate to defeat both Roosevelt and Taft in the 1912 general elections. Speaker Clark had gathered the most delegates in the preconvention direct primaries, and he had the most outstanding Progressive record. But New Jersey Governor Woodrow Wilson was also considered acceptable by many Progressives.

Speaker Clark received more delegate votes on the first ballot without receiving the party's nomination than any candidate of either party had since 1864. Clark's total of 40.6 percent of the delegate votes on the first ballot rose to more than 50 percent on later ballots, but the two-thirds rule kept him from getting the coveted nomination. The Wilson forces were able to prevent Clark from gaining the necessary two-thirds and, finally, on the forty-sixth ballot, Woodrow Wilson was elected the Democratic nominee, a Type D candidate. The Democratic platform was drawn from the Populist Progressive strain and did not reflect the urban orientation the party had hinted it might take. Wilson knew that with Taft and Roosevelt splitting the Republican votes, he needed only to hold the Democratic loyalists to win. Wilson ran a relatively Conservative campaign and ignored most of the Progressive reforms written into the party platform.

The renomination of President Taft by the Republican convention in 1912 exemplified, in much the same fashion as the Harrison nomination had in 1892, the serious difficulty a Type E candidate has in winning re-election. At a Type E convention the incumbent president receives less than 60 percent of the delegate votes on the first ballot, a fairly sure sign that the party is not unified in its support of the incumbent's candidacy. Such a division in support also suggests that the party leaders feel that the president has done a less than satisfactory job during his four years in office. Such was the feeling with William Howard Taft. Even though the four years of Taft's administration had been relatively peaceful and prosperous, the Progressive movement had taken hold of thousands of American voters. When Taft's performance in office failed to meet the expectations of Progressive Republicans, they split off and formed a new party, thus destroying any chance Taft might have had of becoming a two-term president.

Like Benjamin Harrison in 1892, Taft found it difficult to convince American voters that he had performed successfully on the job when large factions within his own party believed he had not. Any incumbent president without the backing of a unified party or a large majority of his own party will find it difficult to convince the nation's electorate that he should be returned to office. With Taft virtually eliminated, the election of 1912 became a contest between Theodore Roosevelt and Woodrow Wilson. Roosevelt was running on a third-party ticket, and no third-party candidate had been a major challenger to the two major parties in the United States since 1860. Third-party candidates are not included in our classification system, so in this race Roosevelt remains unclassified.

As a compromise candidate, Woodrow Wilson was probably not as strong a campaigner as he might have been. The gaping rifts in the Republican party overshadowed the lesser divisions in the Democratic party between the Conservative and Progressive factions, but the Democratic party was not solidly united behind its candidate. In fact, some elements within the party were heatedly opposed to Wilson's nomination.

Wilson had the typical weaknesses of a Type D candidate: he was not the front-runner going into the convention; he was not considered as progressive, nor did he have as many delegate votes, as Speaker of the House Champ Clark. As a candidate who was not nominated until the forty-sixth ballot, he could scarcely be considered a driving, forceful national leader. As a matter of fact, he had been supported in his first political campaign for the governorship of New Jersey by the New Jersey political bosses, who felt he would add a certain amount of respectability to their party ticket.

Wilson's candidacy did, nonetheless, unify the Democratic party sufficiently to defeat the disastrously divided Republican party. The large number of ballots taken to nominate Wilson indicated that there was considerable division of opinion as to which Democrat would provide the most formidable opposition for Theodore Roosevelt. As the least objectionable candidate, Wilson did provide an adequate rallying point for the Democrats as they set forth to defeat both the incumbent President Taft and the insurgent Republican, Theodore Roosevelt.

Their selection was affirmed when Wilson, a Type D candidate, defeated both Taft, a Type E candidate, and Theodore Roosevelt, an unclassified candidate.

CHAPTER FOURTEEN

1884
Cleveland vs. Blaine
TYPE D VS. TYPE F

When James Garfield died on September 19, 1881, from gun-shot wounds received from a mentally deranged office-seeker, Charles J. Guiteau, Chester A. Arthur became president of the United States. Arthur was a former customs collector for the port of New York who had been removed because of a scandal. As the vice-presidential nominee, Arthur was considered a representative of the Stalwart faction of the Republican party. The Stalwarts became deeply disappointed with him, however, when he proceeded to conduct a fair and scandal-free administration and when he moved to institute serious civil service reform. By 1884, Arthur had been seriously weakened by the disaffection of his former constituency, the Stalwarts, yet was unable to win over either of the other two factions, the Half-Breeds or the Republican independents, because of his previous association with the Stalwarts and his previous involvement in New York scandals.

In 1884, the Republicans were split into three major factions. The Stalwarts were headed by Roscoe Conkling, who had controlled the presidency as a private fiefdom during the eight-year tenure of Ulysses S. Grant. It was the Stalwarts who had supported Grant so strongly in 1880 and who were so embittered when they lost to James Garfield. Although Chester Arthur had been one of them, they felt he had betrayed them and their hopes of patronage by presiding over a relatively fair and scandal-free administration. The Dissidents were led by Carl Schurz, the same man who had led the Liberal Republican bolt in 1872. This group, concerned at the lack of honest and efficient government, demanded an end to the odious practice of governmental patronage and the graft and corruption that frequently plagued the federal government. Between the Stalwarts and the Dissidents, or Independent Republicans, were the Moderates or Half-Breeds. The Half-Breeds sought some reforms within the party, mainly those dealing with efficiency and honesty in government, but they supported many of the policies of the Stalwarts such as high tariffs and conservative finance. The leaders of the Half-Breeds were author and future senator Henry Cabot Lodge, President protemp of the U.S. senate George F. Edmunds, and the young Theodore Roosevelt.

The Democrats had not won the presidency since James Buchanan's election in 1856, and the Republicans in 1884 seemed determined to give them another opportunity to run the country. The Republicans were hurt not only by the split within the party over Arthur's presidency, but also by a temporary but extremely severe recession in several of the eastern urban areas.

The 1884 Republican convention became a battle between the incumbent President Chester A. Arthur and the Half-Breed James G. Blaine. Arthur received most of his support from the South, an area the Republicans knew they could not win and, therefore, he was not as strong a competitor as the number of delegate votes he received indicated he might be. Blaine was supported by members of all factions of the party except the Independents. The Independents despised Blaine and vowed to prevent his nomination. The Republican Independents, or Mugwumps as they were frequently called, opposed Blaine's candidacy because they felt that his moral and ethical standing did not fit him for the highest office in the land. Many of the Mugwumps left the Republican party and turned to the Democratic nominee, Grover Cleveland. They were instrumental in winning New York for Cleveland and were, therefore, a critical factor in the outcome of the election.

Throwing aside their incumbent president created an enormous breach in the Republican party. Certain elements within the party were sure to back the incumbent president, either out of personal loyalty or because of patronage they had received.

A serious factional division within the party is inevitable when the incumbent nominee seeks renomination and is refused renomination.

Furthermore, it is difficult for a political party to explain to the American people why it wishes to replace its presidential nominee. If there has not been a serious scandal and if the president's personal life has not been marred by unethical behavior, there would seem to be little reason for a party in power not to continue with the same president. If the party casts its incumbent president aside, it announces its dissatisfaction with his administration. As the party identified with the president and with the Republicans in control of the Senate during the preceding four years and the House of Representatives during two of those four years, the Republican party had to accept some of the blame for the failures of the administration they were seeking to punish by refusing renomination.

The supporters of the candidate who has been refused renomination must be told why he was replaced as the head of the party's ticket and why the entire party should not be held responsible for the failures attributed to the previous administration by elements of the incumbent party itself.

In the face of competition from a large number of parties in 1884, including the Prohibition party, the Greenback party, the Anti-monopoly party, the American party, the Equal Woman's Rights party, the American Prohibition party, and the Republicans, the Democrats attempted to attract votes with a rather nebulous party platform and by presenting a candidate who had a clear image of integrity and honesty. To provide the greatest contrast to the soiled James G. Blaine, the Republican candidate, who was tainted with involvement in a political scandal, the Democrats selected the governor of New York, Grover Cleveland. Cleveland, a popular reformer in New York State, was the leading candidate for the Democratic nomination for the presidency. He received 47.8 percent of the delegate votes on the first ballot and more than two-thirds on the second. Cleveland's popularity was great enough to give the Democratic party a vision of its first presidential victory since 1856. The unity in the party, bolstered by the support of the Mugwumps and the leading independent Republican newspaper, *The New York Times,* gave the Democrats the impetus they needed to win the 1884 presidential election, 4,875,971 to 4,852,234.

Cleveland's nomination indicated that the Democratic party was seeking a compromise candidate, that no overwhelmingly popular leader was available, and that he was as close to being a universally acceptable nominee as the party had. The Democrats were able to begin the 1884 election campaign after their Type D convention with a fairly unified party and with some expectation of victory, knowing that the Republicans had just emerged from a convention that severely damaged the party's unity and disrupted its forces. The Republican party, by repudiating its incumbent in its Type F convention, was probably as divided as it would be until the catastrophe of 1912. The party's presidential incumbent was not renominated, and a large segment of Republican independents left the party in disgust as the party nominated its tarnished knight, James G. Blaine.

CHAPTER FIFTEEN

1972
Nixon vs. McGovern

When political historians twenty years from now look back at the 1972 Democratic and Republican national conventions, the phenomenon they will probably focus on will be the far-reaching reforms undertaken by both parties as a result of their experiences in 1968. Although the reforms in the Republican party did little to affect the party's nominee and probably contributed even less to the eventual success of the party's incumbent president, the reforms in the Democratic party have been viewed by many political observers as critical determinants both in the nomination of George McGovern and in his landslide defeat. The convention reforms of 1972 covered both the selection of delegates and the procedures that would be followed in the convention deliberations.

Supporters of changes in delegate selection processes and convention procedures following the 1968 conventions generally believed the reforms would make the parties more representative, more responsive and, as a consequence, stronger. William B. Welsh, the Democratic party executive director, represented the views of many supporters of convention reform when he suggested that the changed rules brought many new people into the political arena and then kept them within the confines of the two-party political structure. But the opponents of convention reform argued that the delegate selection procedure changes and the convention procedure changes would in fact narrow the appeal of the parties and probably result in the nomination of weaker candidates than under normal circumstances.

By far the most comprehensive changes in convention procedures were effected by the Democrats through two commissions. The first commission, headed first by Senator George McGovern of South Dakota and later by Representative Donald M. Fraser of Minnesota, was concerned with party structure and delegate selection. The second commission, chaired by Representative James G. O'Hara of Michigan, was concerned with the rules governing convention procedures.

There may be arguments as to whether or not the convention reforms made the parties stronger or weaker, but there can be little doubt as to some of their practical effects. There is no doubt that the delegate selection reforms enacted by the Democrats affected the Democratic convention more than the Republican reforms affected the Republican convention. There is also little doubt that a major consequence of the delegate selection procedure changes was an increase in the number of primaries from seventeen in 1968 to twenty-three in 1972. In 1968, 42 percent of the convention votes came from primary states. By 1972, following the delegate selection procedure changes, the percentage of votes from primary states had increased to 63 percent. This meant that by 1972, 1,900 convention votes would come from primary states. Only 1,509 votes were required to nominate a candidate. Theoretically, then, the Democrats could select a nominee for president who would receive all of his convention votes from primary states, which would be a far cry from the conventions of the smoke-filled rooms and the political bosses, who decided on the party's nominee without significant consultation with the rank-and-file party members.

The twenty-three primaries in 1972 turned out to be extraordinarily grueling for the major Democratic contenders. An incredible amount of time, energy, and money was required to maintain momentum and the semblance of a political organization through this divisive and expensive campaign process. Several of the opponents of the convention procedure changes pointed out that the increased number of primaries would probably serve to make the Democratic party even less united than it had been before the conventions and might very well serve to eliminate some of the party's strongest contenders and allow less popular dark-horse candidates to win simply because they were able to survive the long process.

A dark-horse candidate, it was pointed out, could remain in the running even though he might do very poorly in the first few primaries simply because the expectations of his performance would be rather low. A candidate might lose but still come out ahead in a primary if he did better than was expected by the media and the political pros. A candidate might be expected to receive 10 percent of the vote and then be treated as a victor when he received 15 percent of the vote. In contrast, a front-runner would have to win almost every primary or do very well in every primary to avoid elimination simply because he would not meet the expectations surrounding his front-runner position. It would be almost an impossible task, it was frequently suggested, to expect one candidate to win all twenty-three of the primaries. But if the front-runner did not win all or almost all of the twenty-three primaries, he might be effectively eliminated even though he was in effect, performing quite well.

This was certainly the case with Senator Edmund Muskie of Maine. Under the old delegate selection rules, it is generally conceded, Senator Muskie would have had the nomination locked up before the primaries even began because of the broad support he enjoyed among Democratic leaders. But when the delegate selection process changes shifted power to the grass-roots level, Muskie's strength was so seriously diluted that he was forced to compete in most of the primaries in order to prove that he was capable of winning the Democratic nomination. Inasmuch as only about 37 percent of the delegates were not selected through primaries, Muskie had to win a substantial number of primary votes if he hoped to capture the nomination.

Muskie's situation was in stark contrast to that of Vice-President Hubert Humphrey in 1968. Humphrey succeeded in capturing the Democratic nomination without entering or, of course, winning a single primary.

Votes from presidential primary states did not necessarily represent solid blocs committed to any one particular candidate at the 1972 Democratic national convention. Only California,

Massachusetts, Oregon, and South Dakota were represented by winner-take-all slates; that is, only those four states had primaries where the candidate who won a majority of the votes in the primary received all of the state's delegate votes at the convention.

Most of the states using the primary election method of delegate selection choose their delegates by means of either congressional district apportionment or at-large selections. Thus it was possible for one candidate to win all of the primary elections and still not be guaranteed the nomination. It would have been possible in 1972 for one candidate to win a majority in all of the twenty-three primary contests and still come out two hundred and fifty delegate votes short of the number needed to gain the nomination. Most of the delegates, approximately 75 to 80 percent, were chosen at the congressional district level. The others were selected by at-large procedures. In most state contests, the candidate who won a particular congressional district would get that district's delegates, and the candidate who won the majority statewide would receive the at-large delegates. It was possible for one candidate to win heavily in a few congressional districts and thereby win the at-large delegates but still not win a majority in most of the congressional districts. Senator Humphrey performed this feat in Ohio.

Before the 1972 convention reforms, many of the delegates to the national party conventions were selected by state party officials. But the McGovern/Fraser Commission guidelines established that at least 75 percent of the delegates would have to be selected at the congressional district level. The McGovern/Fraser guidelines also stipulated that representatives of minority groups, women, and youth would have to be "in reasonable proportion to their representation in the party as a whole in that state." One of the guidelines the credentials committee at the Democratic national convention used was the demand that a convention slate not be accepted if it had fewer than 40 percent women on it, a stipulation that necessitated a dramatic change from the 1968 Democratic convention, when only 16 percent of the delegates were women.

Besides this increase of at least 24 percent more women at the convention, the credentials committee pointed out that the percentage of minorities would have to go up. In 1968, only 5.5 percent of the Democratic convention delegates were black, although 20 percent of the Democratic vote in 1968 was accounted for by blacks, and blacks make up approximately 11 percent of the nation's population.

The changes that increased the number of young people, women, and minorities at the Democratic national convention so dramatically were a significant boon to the candidacy of Senator George McGovern. But a hidden boomerang effect was also obvious in the dramatic changes. The attraction that Senator McGovern had for many young people, owing to his reliance on reforms to gain support at many of the open-party caucuses, and his decision not to rely on the strength of the old-line party leadership alienated a number of long-time Democratic professionals. The reforms also limited by necessity the number of traditional Democratic leaders who could bring their full contingents to Miami Beach with them. Probably the best-publicized of these exclusion moves was that which excluded Mayor Richard Daley of Chicago from the convention. The 1972 Democratic national convention was the first convention since 1956 in which Mayor Daley had not played a prominent role.

At the Democratic convention, groups such as the Woman's Political Caucus, the Congressional Black Caucus, the National Farmer's Union, and Common Cause attempted to monitor the seating of delegates and file challenges whenever they felt the rules of the McGovern/Fraser Commission were being violated. In all, the credentials committee was faced with eighty-two challenges to one thousand, two hundred and eighty-nine delegates from thirty states and one territory, that is, almost 42 percent of the delegates were challenged by some person or group and faced the scrutiny of the credentials committee.

The impact of the O'Hara Commission on rules was also evident at the 1972 Democratic convention. The purpose of the O'Hara Commission was to streamline the procedures at the convention, to broaden the capabilities of delegates to participate in convention procedures, and to increase their level of understanding about these procedures. Several of the most noticeable changes in convention rules were the following: Instead of being called by alphabetical order, the states were called according to a drawing of lots; the candidacies of favorite sons were eliminated; and, in an attempt to speed the normally slow convention processes, a limit of fifteen total minutes for speeches and any floor demonstrations was placed on nominating and seconding speeches.

The Republican national convention in 1972 adopted ten new recommendations designed to make the party more representative of the general electorate. But while the Democratic selection procedures played an important role in the determination of the party's nominee, and therefore received significant publicity, the Republican changes had little effect on the selection of the party's nominee and received little publicity. The Republican modification of delegate selection procedures was similar to that of the Democrats. It was concerned with making certain that the proportion of minorities, women, and young people at the conventions would be relatively proportional to the proportion of women, minorities, and young people in the country, as a whole. This attempt, however, was more informal than the Democrats' and was not as far reaching.

As the primary campaigns got underway in January of 1972, the Republican party prospects for a Type B convention appeared almost certain. The Republicans had an incumbent President who was not only relatively popular but who in the minds of many Americans was successfully winding down an unpopular war in Southeast Asia and was promoting the cause of world peace with diplomatic initiatives in both China and Russia. On the other hand, the prospects of an A convention on the part of the Democrats seemed bleak. And, of course, a Type A convention was the only hope the Democrats had of defeating the incumbent Republican President. Since 1864, the only incumbent president who was renominated without massive defections in his own party and went on to lose the general election was Herbert Hoover in 1932. He was also the only Type B candidate to run against a Type A candidate.

It was generally acknowledged in January, 1972, that the

front runner by several lengths was Senator Edmund Muskie of Maine, who had been the vice presidential nominee in 1968. Muskie was so far ahead that a Type C nomination, similar to the one in 1968, appeared likely. The conventional wisdom in January, 1972, suggested that no Democratic candidate possessed anywhere near the voter appeal of Senator Muskie. He had the endorsements of a number of U. S. senators and several prominent governors. The general feeling appeared to be that if Muskie did falter, which at that time appeared unlikely, the party would probably splinter, and the result would be a multi-ballot convention which would give the party a Type D nominee. In either case, the theory suggests the incumbent president would be able to win re-election. A multi-ballot convention seemed likely if the party moved away from Muskie, because at one time or another twenty-two different candidates had expressed a desire to be the Democratic party's nominee for president.[1] It seemed unlikely in January that if Muskie faltered, any one of these candidates would be able to pick up the pieces and capture the lion's share of Senator Muskie's support.

Senator Muskie's position, though, was not as secure as it had first appeared. In fact, until Senator Muskie formally announced his candidacy, the leader in most public opinion polls was Senator Hubert Humphrey of Minnesota, the former vice-president. By the time the last nationwide survey was taken before the New Hampshire primary, Muskie had actually fallen behind Humphrey as the preferred candidate for the Democratic party's nomination. Muskie's unimpressive showing in the primary elections therefore should not have come as much of a shock to most knowledgeable political observers who could see from the nationwide opinion polls that he was not as far ahead in the race for the Democratic presidential nomination as his list of prominent supporters indicated he was.

[1]The twenty-two Democratic presidential contenders were: nine senators: Muskie, Humphrey, Jackson, Hughes, Hartke, Bayh, Proxmire, McGovern, and Harris; one former senator, Eugene McCarthy; five congressmen: Mills, Mink, Chisholm, Fauntroy, and Hays; one governor, Wallace; one former governor, Sanford; two mayors, Lindsay and Yorty; one former mayor, Stokes; one anti-poverty worker, Cole; and one national committeeman, Channing Phillips.

Of the twenty-two candidates who at some time announced they would seek the Democratic presidential nomination, only seven tried to put together truly national campaigns. Of these seven, one, Mayor John Lindsay of New York City, fell by the wayside immediately following the Wisconsin primary. His campaign started late and depended primarily on a national concern for urban problems and his own charisma. He received an early boost by his second-place showing at the Arizona state convention, the nation's first. His strategy was to capture third place in Florida, come in a strong second or perhaps even first in Wisconsin, and to win Massachusetts and California. But a poor showing in Florida and a disappointing showing in Wisconsin—he came in sixth place—forced him out of the campaign. Lindsay released his Arizona delegates and ended up at Miami Beach as an uncommitted delegate.

Representative Shirley Chisholm based her campaign on an appeal to women and, to a lesser extent, blacks. Her support among blacks was never very broad except among the young. She received few endorsements from influential black leaders and her appeal to liberal women was seriously diluted by the support given to Senator McGovern. Nevertheless, she saw the primaries through and even played a key role in the stop-McGovern strategy just prior to the convention.

Senator Henry Jackson of Washington state was billed as "the different Democrat." Of all the candidates Jackson was the one most closely identified with the military. As the campaign progressed, Jackson became Governor Wallace's principal opponent for votes from the Democratic right. He received a big boost with his third-place showing in Florida, but after Florida his campaign never again got off the ground. After the Florida primary, Jackson withdrew from active campaigning and remained little more than a favorite son until the unexpected last-minute withdrawals of Humphrey and Muskie threw several hundred delegate votes into his camp at the convention.

If Senator McGovern was the candidate who was most favored by the delegate selection reforms, Senator Muskie was the candidate who was probably most severely hurt by them. Muskie began as a centrist unity candidate, but he never seemed to catch on with the voters, who appeared to be in a mood of protest as they opted for Senator McGovern and Governor Wallace. Whereas McGovern, understanding the impact of the new delegate selection procedures, emphasized his grass-roots organization, Senator Muskie neglected his grass-roots organization and depended to a much greater extent on big-name endorsements. Muskie's strategy probably would have been successful prior to 1972. But the dramatic changes in the delegate selection procedures made his campaign strategy almost totally ineffective.

The fact that a large number of prominent Democratic governors and senators could endorse Muskie while the rank and file preferred another candidate is nothing new in Democratic politics. In April, 1952, a Gallup survey of Democratic county chairmen indicated that fully 48 percent of those who replied believed that Governor Adlai Stevenson could beat Dwight Eisenhower. By a wide margin however, these same Democratic county chairmen said that Senator Estes Kefauver of Tennessee would lose. The last poll of voters before the Democratic convention, however, indicated that Kefauver was preferred by the nation's Democrats 45 percent to Stevenson's 12 percent. In Stevenson's case in 1952, the delegate selection procedures were such that the preferences of the Democratic party leaders were crucial to his nomination. The dramatic effect of the changes in the delegate selection process by 1972 becomes evident when we see that Senator Muskie, who was clearly the favorite candidate of the Democratic party leaders, had become little more than an also-ran by the time of the national convention.

The chief beneficiary of Senator Muskie's decline was Hubert Humphrey, the party's titular leader. Senator Humphrey, because of his position as the party's former vice-president, had considerable latent support from party leaders. He had earned much sympathy because of his dramatic campaign in 1968 and his close-as-a-whisker loss to Richard Nixon. Humphrey was a centrist by 1972 standards, but he still maintained the liberal reputation he had earned in the late 1950's and early 1960's with his strong proposals to promote the causes of labor, minorities, and the elderly. Humphrey's association with Lyndon Johnson and the Vietnam war cut him off from some of his previous liberal support, and the civil rights stands that brought him his minority following were counterbalanced to a certain extent by pressures from the Wallace reaction. Humphrey suffered from a lack of money and organization and frequently showed signs of the generation gap. He was never fully able to shake the image of the "Old Pol," which stuck to him throughout the campaign. Nevertheless, he remained the strongest alternative to the McGovern candidacy until the very end.

The basic theme of both the McGovern and Wallace campaigns was protest. Both candidates agreed that the federal government had grown too remote from the average citizen and that the "little man" deserved a fair shake, both in terms of taxation policy and in terms of his ability to influence the workings of the political system. On social issues and foreign policy, though, candidates Wallace and McGovern were poles apart. During the primaries the impact of this protest vote demonstrated the similarity of the appeal that McGovern and Wallace had for many of America's voters. As the primaries progressed, it became obvious that the McGovern-Wallace appeal was probably the single strongest appeal of any candidate or team of candidates. It was frequently pointed out by pollsters that McGovern and Wallace often were deriving support from the same basic constituency.

The primaries began on March 7 in New Hampshire. The only major candidates entered were Senator Muskie of Maine and Senator McGovern. Originally it was expected that New Hampshire would be an easy and overwhelming victory for Senator Muskie. As it turned out, Muskie did win in New Hampshire but only after a surprisingly close fight with Senator McGovern. On March 14th, Florida voters went to the polls. Governor Wallace dominated the election, as did the issue of busing school children. Senator Humphrey, with less than half as many votes as Governor Wallace, came in second; Senator Jackson was third; Senator Muskie fourth; and Mayor Lindsay narrowly edged out Senator McGovern for fifth place.

The impact of the Florida primary on the candidacies of Senators Muskie and Humphrey indicates very clearly the phenomenon that was mentioned earlier in this chapter. Muskie, who came in fourth in Florida and first in New Hampshire, was considered now to be almost certainly out of the running for the presidential nomination, although in both instances he defeated Senator McGovern, whose star was just beginning to rise. In New Hampshire, even though Muskie won, he did not win with as large a majority as had been expected. Senator McGovern was expected to lose but lost with a smaller margin of defeat than was expected. So, New Hampshire became a loss for the man who won it and a victory of sorts for the man who lost it. In Florida, Senator Muskie again was expected to do better than he did. By coming in fourth, Senator Muskie did significantly better than Senator McGovern but he had been expected to do even better. McGovern performed about as expected in Florida, and his bandwagon was not slowed to any significant extent. After the Florida primary the Muskie bandwagon appeared to be grinding to a halt.

On March 21st in Illinois, Senator Muskie won his second primary out of the three he had entered, but again his victory was unimpressive. Muskie's victory in Illinois signaled the approaching end of his candidacy. So, even though Muskie had won two victories out of the first three primaries, he was effectively eliminated from contention because his victories had not been as impressive as had been expected.

Because of the delegate selection procedure changes, a candidate such as Senator Muskie, who could easily have received the nomination under the 1968 procedures by competing in only a select few primaries, was eliminated in 1972 because he was forced to do battle in almost every primary to gain the necessary number of delegate votes.

The Wisconsin primary on April 4th gave McGovern his first primary victory. Surprising to many commentators was the showing of Governor Wallace, who came in second. Both Mayor Lindsay and Senator Muskie were, for all practical purposes, eliminated after the Wisconsin primary. In the Massachusetts primary, held on April 25, Senator McGovern scored a sweeping victory.

A fitting example of the type of election year 1972 was to be for the Democrats and the type of convention that was to be held in Miami Beach is the fact that the president of the Massachusetts Historical Society was a delegate to the Miami convention, while the mayor of Boston, Kevin White, was not. In the Pennsylvania primary, also held on April 25, Hubert Humphrey received strong labor support and won a decisive victory. Governor Wallace came in second and Senator McGovern third. Even with the support of Pennsylvania's governor, Senator Muskie could do no better than fourth. With this fourth-place finish, Muskie ended his active primary campaigning, even though he vowed to stay in the race for the Democratic nomination.

On May 2, Senator Humphrey won a very narrow victory over Senator McGovern in the Ohio primary election. On the same day in Indiana Senator Humphrey scored a narrow victory over Governor Wallace. In Alabama, Wallace was an easy victor, and in Washington, D.C. the District's lone representative in Congress, Walter Fauntroy, won the primary against a slate headed by national committeeman Channing Phillips.

On May 4, Tennessee held its presidential primary and gave Wallace his largest victory so far. Governor Wallace's victory in North Carolina dealt a serious blow to the hopes of former North Carolina governor and Duke University president, Terry Sanford.

Both Nebraska and West Virginia held their primaries on May 9. In Nebraska, Senator McGovern, with the support of both insurgents and regulars, showed that he could surmount the identification with "Amnesty, Abortion, and Acid" and won a narrow victory over Senator Humphrey. West Virginia was Humphrey territory in 1972 and George Wallace was decisively defeated there. On May 15, Governor Wallace was critically wounded by a would-be assassin in Maryland. On the 16th, influenced perhaps by the events of the day before, Governor Wallace's forces won a two-to-one victory over Senator McGovern in Michigan. On the same day, Governor Wallace won a substantial victory over Senator Humphrey in the state in which he had been shot.

On May 23, Senator McGovern won a five-to-two victory

over Governor Wallace in Oregon with Senator Humphrey third. On the same day, Rhode Island gave McGovern a two-to-one margin of victory over Senator Muskie. Again Humphrey was a close third.

On June 6, South Dakota, California, New Jersey, and New Mexico held primaries. Senator McGovern, for all practical purposes, assured himself of the presidential nomination by winning all four primaries. The California primary was particularly important because it was a winner-take-all primary. Unlike many of the primaries in which candidates were selected on a district-wide basis and the candidate who won a majority state-wide would not necessarily win all of the delegates, California had a plurality take-all system, that is, the candidate who received the most votes won all of the state's delegates.

New York held the nation's last official primary on June 20. The election was a significant victory for Senator McGovern over a badly splintered field. As the primaries drew to a close at the end of June, Senator McGovern was leading the field with ten victories (only three of which came before May 23 and before George Wallace was effectively eliminated from the race); Senator Humphrey had four victories; Governor Wallace six victories; Senator Muskie two victories; and Walter Fauntroy won the last remaining primary in the District of Columbia.

While the primaries were catching the nation's spotlight, many of the states that did not hold primaries were holding statewide conventions to select their delegates to the national convention. McGovern was the plurality winner of the non-primary states, but he did not do as well as in the primaries. The biggest loser in terms of delegate votes from the convention states was Governor Wallace. Governor Wallace won the second largest number of primary victories but won in only one convention state, Texas. His lack of an organization that could compete effectively with those of McGovern, Muskie, and Humphrey in the convention states was a serious drawback to his candidacy.

As the primary season drew to a close, it appeared that the worst fears of the critics of the McGovern/Fraser Commission were being realized. Sixteen of the twenty-three primaries had been won by the two most extreme candidates, Senator Mc-Govern and Governor Wallace. The contention that the strongest, most moderate candidates would be shunted aside by the more extreme candidates and those with small but cohesive followings was apparently coming true. By the end of June, it had become obvious that the name of the new primary game was survival. And the survival game was played best by candidates who had cohesive followings and whose appeal was focused and long-lasting.

For a front-runner like Edmund Muskie, the new procedures spelled almost certain disaster. Muskie was forced to go the primary route because he knew that 63 percent of the delegates at the 1972 convention would be selected in state primaries. But being a centrist candidate, he was also the candidate who was most likely to suffer when the number of candidates began to proliferate. Each time a new candidate entered the fold, he/she appeared to take a small segment of Senator Muskie's constituency. The candidates on the extreme edges of the party were less likely to lose their more devoted followers and thus suffered relatively little in comparison with Muskie when the number of potential presidential candidates began to approach twenty.

Muskie, and to a certain extent Humphrey, appeared to be playing by the rules that had been operative in 1968. Muskie and Humphrey apparently did not perceive as clearly as did McGovern the dramatic changes that the new procedures would make in the actual selection of the Democratic presidential nominee. Thus, instead of building a strong grass-roots organization, the Muskie forces spent considerable time courting the party leaders and the traditional Democratic heavyweights, who ended up with relatively little power at the convention. The McGovern forces concentrated their energy on building a strong primary organization and the stamina to withstand the punishment of the primary campaigns.

One consequence of this reorganization of traditional delegate selection procedures was the belief on the part of many Democrats that the best candidate had not won. The feeling from many quarters was that the victories of Senator Mc-Govern, seven of which had come very late in the primary campaign, did not truly reflect the wishes of a great mass of Democratic voters.

It is probably true that Senator McGovern would not have received the Democratic presidential nomination had not the McGovern/Fraser Commission reformed the delegate selection procedures between 1968 and 1972. It is almost as certainly true that under the procedures operative in 1968 Senator Muskie would have received the nomination, because he could have relied on the support of most of the party officials who count in a convention in which only 42 percent of the delegates are selected in state primaries.

Because McGovern went on to win the Democratic presidential nomination with approximately 57 percent of the delegate votes on the first ballot, some modifications must be made in our theory of conflict and harmony to account for the fact that McGovern, a Type A nominee, went on to lose in a landslide to a Type B nominee, incumbent President Richard Nixon. Our theory of conflict and harmony assumes that all of the candidates competing for their party's nomination are competing under essentially the same rules. It also assumes that the changes from year to year in delegate selection procedures are only minimal. If dramatic changes take place, such as those which occurred between 1968 and 1972, we may expect the results of the convention to be thrown off and perhaps even invalidated as far as the theory is concerned, because the candidates are operating under different sets of rules.

It was fairly obvious during the primary campaigns that Senator Muskie was operating under a different set of assumptions than Senator McGovern was. It is also fairly obvious that Senator McGovern's chances for the Democratic nomination would have been almost non-existent if the delegate selection procedures had not been changed so drastically. Because of the McGovern/Fraser Commission reforms and their impact on the probability that each candidate was operating under the same set of rules, we found the delegate selection procedures operative in the convention itself to be abnormal. We found, for example, that the demographic make-up of the delegates to the 1972 convention was dramatically different from that of the

1968 convention delegates.[2] By 1976, the reforms put into effect between 1968 and 1972 will have been internalized by prospective candidates and we will probably find that by 1976 the same rules will apply to all candidates because they all will be familiar with the way the rules operate in both a theoretical and a practical sense. We will probably find that no candidate in 1976 will be as advantaged by the rule changes as Senator McGovern was in 1972. It appears to us, then, that Senator McGovern was a candidate separate from the regular Democratic tradition. Probably most indicative of this trend is the fact that Senator Muskie won two out of the first three primaries, yet was considered almost out of the running by the time the third primary had run its course. While Muskie was winning two of the first three primaries, Senator McGovern was coming in second in the first, a very poor sixth in the second, and not even competing in the third; yet McGovern was winning support as an increasingly viable candidate.

Apart from the fact that McGovern received the nomination largely because of the modification in delegate selection procedures, and the likelihood that under the old procedures Senator Muskie would have won the nomination with either a Type C or a Type D convention, the 1972 convention was a relatively predictable Type A convention. On the first ballot, Senator McGovern received 1,715.35 votes out of a possible 3,016. A Type A convention, we have noted, should produce the best mixture of conflict and harmony. The Type A candidate cannot so totally control a convention as to force extreme measures on unwilling delegates, yet his control over the convention is strong enough to give his party the same basic sense of direction that his own campaign had. Normally the Type A

[2]	% of 1968 Delegates	% of 1972 Delegates
Women	13	40
Blacks	6	15
Income less than $10,000	13	27
Under age 30	4	21
College education	43	52

*See John W. Soule and Wilma McGrath, "The Effects of Increased Democracy in Presidential Nomination Politics: The Democrats, 1972," unpublished paper, San Diego State University, 1973, p. 6.

convention has been the culmination of a long, intense struggle that continued until the beginning of the convention itself. This long struggle normally engenders a high sense of vitality in the party as well as the possibility of polarization if the winning candidate is not careful to soothe the feelings of the defeated contenders. Two of the most important decision-making areas for the successful nominee are those relating to writing the platform and choosing the vice-presidential nominee. Both of these decisions give the presidential nominee an opportunity to bring the party back into the harmonious state from which it may have been wrenched by the primary elections and campaigns.

The 1972 Democratic platform was of the general type one would expect from a Type A convention. The ideas and ideals of Senator McGovern provided the general sense of direction, but the specific platform statements were far more moderate than those which had been suggested and supported by many of McGovern's leading supporters. The toned-down platform was designed to meet the objections of Senators Muskie and Humphrey and to suggest to all of the competing candidates that Senator McGovern was quite willing to move the platform to a moderate stance acceptable to as many of the candidates and to as much of the convention as possible.

The one candidate with whom no reasonable compromise appeared to be effected was Governor Wallace of Alabama. Frequently during the course of the convention McGovern supporters joined with the supporters of Muskie and Humphrey and other centrist candidates to defeat platform proposals that under other circumstances McGovern might have supported. In a Type B or a Type C convention, the McGovern forces' proposals for liberalizing abortion laws and instituting relatively high-level minimum income supports nationwide might have passed. But in a Type A convention the McGovern forces did not have the strength to ignore the wishes of the more moderate candidates.

But there appeared to be no effective way for the McGovern forces to join hands with the Wallace supporters by moderating the McGovern proposals enough to make them acceptable to the Wallace supporters. The Wallace forces lost a series of voice votes and suffered more consistent defeats than did any other faction. Normally in a Type A convention we would expect the convention's nominee to be able to reconcile the differences of all the major factions within the party. Such was the case with John Kennedy in 1960 and with Richard Nixon in 1968, but it certainly was not the case with Senator McGovern in 1972. McGovern's selection as the nominee, as we pointed out earlier, was probably a consequence of the changes in delegate selection procedures. These changes made possible the selection of a candidate from one of the two extreme ends of the party. Under normal circumstances, the selection of a candidate from one of the two extremes of the party in a Type A convention would be almost impossible. But once such a nominee is chosen, it is almost impossible for him to accommodate both the wishes of his own followers and those of candidates from the other extreme wing of the party. A candidate in the middle might be able to accomplish a significant accommodation with both extremes in the party by giving a little to each side. But the McGovern forces felt that they had already given ground when they moderated their stances to conform to the wishes of the centrists. To go further and conform to the wishes of the Wallace supporters was asking a bit too much.

Because the delegates at the convention were often selected at district conventions and state-wide primaries rather than by political bosses, they were a far more independent group than is normally seen at political party conventions, and at times Senator McGovern had trouble keeping his own forces in line. Having to struggle to maintain control over his own followers handicapped McGovern's efforts to reach an accommodation with Wallace's supporters that certainly would have increased the chances that they would join forces with him in a united presidential campaign once the convention was over.

Two other factors demonstrate the complex effects of the delegate selection reforms on the 1972 Democratic national convention. One factor was the fact that polls taken just before the Democratic national convention showed that only 30 percent of Democratic voters wanted Senator McGovern to be the party's nominee—after McGovern had won ten of the twenty-three primaries and was fairly assured of being the party's nominee.

Another important factor to consider is the existence of significant differences between the preferences of delegates from primary states and those of delegates from non-primary states. For example, from the primary states Senator McGovern received 1,311.8 votes out of a total possible of 2,017, or approximately 65 percent of the votes of delegates from primary states. Senator Jackson received 11.45 percent, Governor Wallace 15.45 percent, and the other candidates split the remainder. From non-primary states, in contrast, Senator McGovern received only 403.55 votes out of a possible 999 votes, or approximately 40 percent of the delegate votes. Senator Jackson had 30.3 percent of the votes from non-primary states, while Governor Wallace had 7 percent, Shirley Chisholm 8.5 percent, and Senator Humphrey approximately 5 percent. The remaining votes went either to Terry Sanford, to Wilbur Mills, or to Edmund Muskie.

As we mentioned earlier, the two major areas of compromise for a Type A nominee are the platform and the selection of a vice-presidential nominee. In 1972, the Democratic Type A nominee, George McGovern, went to considerable lengths to reach as comprehensive and as broad a series of compromises as possible with the factions of the party that had opposed his nomination. He was relatively successful in reaching working agreements with most segments of the party, with the notable exception of the Wallace faction.

The second major area of compromise was the selection of a vice-president. The man selected by Senator McGovern to be his running-mate was Thomas Eagleton of Missouri. Eagleton was a Catholic, whereas McGovern was a Protestant, and Eagleton had strong ties with labor, whereas McGovern found himself increasingly estranged from the leaders of many of the nation's labor unions. Senator Eagleton was younger than Senator McGovern, and his basic appeal was earthy and blue-collar—oriented, while Senator McGovern's appeal was much more intellectual in nature.

As we would expect from a Type A convention, Senator

Eagleton's nomination as the vice-presidential candidate was seen to be a means of plugging what appeared to be serious gaps in Senator McGovern's coalition. Unfortunately for the Democratic ticket, it was discovered within weeks after the convention that Senator Eagleton had undergone shock treatments several years earlier for a health condition. Reacting to widespread demands from his supporters, Senator McGovern decided to change vice presidential candidates.

When George McGovern asked Thomas Eagleton to remove himself from the Democratic party's national ticket, after Eagleton's disclosure that he had undergone electro-shock treatments for severe depression, the carefully constructed compromise made possible by Eagleton's presence on the ticket began to fall apart.

Never before in history had a presidential nominee asked his vice-president to remove himself from the party's national ticket. At two different times in the nation's history something has happened to a party's vice-presidential candidate so that the original candidate was not on the ticket when election day rolled around. But in the first instance the vice-presidential nominee, Senator Silas Wright of New York, simply refused to accept the nomination with John Tyler, and in the second instance, President William Taft's vice-presidential candidate died just a few weeks before the election. In neither case was the outcome of the election seriously affected by the vice-president's absence from the ticket. But in this instance, when we are dealing with a Type A nominee whose major strengths are the twin factors of harmony and vitality, the removal of the vice-presidential nominee was tantamount to removing one of the linchpins in the compromise machinery.

Historically, the power of the Type A nominee has been rooted in the vitality that a hard-fought primary brought into the election campaign and the harmony achieved at the convention when the nominee was able to reconcile the competing factions and bring them together in a strongly unified party. Certainly this was the case, theoretically, with the Democrats in 1972. The existence of a large number of Democratic candidates competing for the presidency and the high caliber of those candidates indicated that there was widespread belief on the part of Democratic leaders that the incumbent Republican president could be defeated.

The broad and detailed reforms initiated by the McGovern/Fraser Commission on Delegate Selection Procedures, though, modified the rules of the primary game so that the primaries in 1972 were run on a different basis than primaries had been in previous years. One candidate, George McGovern, was able to work the new delegate selection procedures to his own advantage and overcome candidates who had broader support within the party and who certainly did not arouse the animosity toward their candidacy that McGovern experienced. Especially toward the end of the 1972 primary campaign, the feeling among the various candidates grew heated. Part of this heat was probably generated by the conviction on the part of many Democrats that the party's best potential candidate was not going to be nominated at the convention. In fact, many Democrats believed the party had been captured, partly as a result of the reforms in delegate selection procedures, by a candidate whose position was at the extreme left wing of the party. Thus, the Democratic party came into the convention with considerable vitality generated by the optimistic belief on the part of many Democrats that the President could be defeated and by the competitive primaries from which the candidates had just emerged. The convention itself was a typical Type A convention with the nominee Senator McGovern making the requisite compromises on both the platform and the vice-presidency. But because he was a candidate of the left, McGovern was unable to reconcile major differences with the factions of the right headed by Governor Wallace.

The nomination of Senator Eagleton was a key element in the compromise structure. The platform compromises were one part of the structure, and the compromise on the vice-presidential nomination was the second part. The vice-presidential nominee had to be someone who could placate the factions to the right of McGovern and counterbalance McGovern's lack of constituencies in some areas with a following of his own. When

Eagleton was dropped, though, the delicate compromise that had been worked out was shattered.

Besides the shadows that dropping Senator Eagleton cast on McGovern's image as a principled and humanistic candidate, Eagleton's dismissal from the ticket created a problem for the McGovern forces who were forced then to come up with a compromise candidate who could bring into the presidential campaign the same forces to which Eagleton had some appeal. Sargent Shriver, then serving as ambassador to France, was not able to fill this compromise gap, because his candidacy was seen by many as more of a desperate effort by the McGovern forces to entice a "name" candidate onto the ticket than an effort to effect a compromise with the factions that were in essential disagreement with McGovern. It also appeared that Shriver lacked the appeal to some of the ethnic groups and labor groups that would have been needed to effect a truly viable compromise that could unify all elements of the party.

The modifications in the delegate selection rules, combined with the Eagleton affair after the convention, acted as a one-two punch that crippled the impact of the Type A convention. The modification of delegate selection rules hampered the vitality that normally accrues to the party from a competitive primary campaign, because McGovern was seen by many to have received the nomination under slightly unfair circumstances. The Eagleton affair effectively wrecked the makeup of the necessary compromise package by eliminating one of the two major compromises that the Type A presidential nominee is forced to make.

Past convention history indicates that when supporters of a candidate for the presidential nomination believe, rightly or wrongly, that their man has been cheated out of the nomination, party cohesion will be next to impossible to achieve. At the 1972 convention, because the delegate selection reforms were felt by many to be responsible for the failures of Senators Humphrey and Muskie, the benefits that accrue to a Type A nominee were partially nullified.

The question that many of the non-McGovern supporters undoubtedly were asking themselves at the convention was whether or not McGovern could have been nominated under the rules that were effective in 1968. And, if McGovern could not have been nominated under these rules, what would the 1972 result have been? Would their candidate have been the party's nominee if the rules had not been changed by the McGovern/Fraser Commission?

Most delegates were certainly aware that the delegate selection procedures in 1972 differed in three important ways from those in 1968. First, a sort of loose quota now existed regarding the age, the sex, and the ethnic background of the delegates to the Democratic national convention; this sort of quota did not exist in 1968. Second, the 1972 rules saw the transfer of control over the makeup of the delegations going to state conventions and local caucuses from party officials, in some states, to the voters themselves. And third, as we mentioned earlier, the 1972 delegate selection reforms increased the number of primaries from seventeen to twenty-three.

To gauge the consequences of these changes, let us go back first to 1968 and compare the results of that year and the format of that year to the results of 1972. If we compare the results of the voting on the minority Viet Nam plank, in the binding primary states, the non-binding primary states, and the convention states, we see that the differences are striking indeed. The vote for the binding primary states was 207.5 for the majority and 420 for the minority. In other words, the delegates from binding primary states favored the minority Viet Nam plank by more than two to one. From the non-binding primary states, the delegates favored the majority plank 298.25 to 122.25. So we see that in the non-binding states, the majority plank was favored approximately two and a half to one.

If we now proceed to the convention states, those states which do not have primaries, we see that the majority plank won 1,062 to only 499, approximately two to one in favor of the majority plank. It is clear that the use of binding primaries was conducive to support for the minority plank. In the binding primary states the insurgents won on the minority plank more than two to one, while in the non-binding primary states and in the convention states the minority plank lost more than two to one.

If we repeat the same breakdown for the presidential balloting, we find very similar results. In the binding primary states, Senator Humphrey received 239 votes to 262 for Senator McCarthy and 129 for others. In the non-binding primary states, Humphrey received 332.75 votes to 72.5 votes for McCarthy, and 21.75 abstaining or voting for someone else, that is, even though McCarthy won in the binding primary states, he lost by more than four to one in the non-binding primary states.

In the convention states Humphrey had 1,188.5 votes to only 266.5 votes for McCarthy and 110 votes either abstaining or voting for someone else. So McCarthy went from a slight victory in the states with binding primaries to a defeat of more than six to one in the convention states. We then see a pattern similar to that which existed in the voting on the Viet Nam plank, in that in the states lacking binding primaries, the traditional big city machine-labor union-south-coalition functioned quite well.

It is true that the influence of these traditional blocs was already somewhat on the decline within the party, and it is true that Senator McGovern had a significantly better organization than Senator McCarthy did. Nevertheless, it is relatively safe to assume that the regulars in the party would have continued to play a dominant, if not quite so overwhelming, role, in a convention conducted under the old rules.

The increase in the number of direct binding primaries was important to the McGovern candidacy for several reasons. First, a candidate running for his party's presidential nomination has normally had several options. If he was relatively unknown or had difficulty convincing party leaders that he could be a strong candidate, he could enter the primaries and prove himself by winning against difficult odds. In a few cases, a win against overwhelming odds could set off a bandwagon, as happened with Senator John F. Kennedy after the West Virginia primary in 1960. On the other hand, to a candidate who was already well known and had a large following, entering primaries often seemed an unnecessary risk. Loss in a major primary could destroy a candidacy, as Harold Stassen found out in Oregon in 1948.

On the other hand, the primaries yielded only a few hundred delegates, and a sweep of the primaries could not guarantee a candidate's nomination if the party leaders were determined to stop him, as Senator Kefauver found out in 1952. It often seemed safer for the front-runner, therefore, to concentrate on building a huge lead in the convention states and thus either become the candidate of the party leaders, or attempt to round up delegates at conventions which were sometimes held years before the national party conventions, as Senator Goldwater did in 1964.

The increase in the number of primaries under the new McGovern/Fraser rules upset the normal calculations of the presidential candidates. A major candidate was now forced to enter the primaries because fully 63 percent of the delegates were selected in states holding primaries. The increase in the number of primaries dramatically expanded the opportunity for established candidates to kill each other off, and for attractive unknown candidates to maintain momentum and pick up the pieces after the major candidates had eliminated each other. It is literally impossible for two, three, or perhaps four major candidates to win all of the primaries. By failing to meet the expectations established for them by the media, major candidates can be effectively eliminated even though they may actually win or do quite well in primaries. Because expectations are low for non-major candidates to begin with, it is much easier for them to survive the primaries than it is for the front-runners. It is probably safe to assume that without the new delegate selection procedures, Senator McGovern would never have acquired enough popularity to win the nomination. He would, most likely, have been the vice-presidential nominee on a ticket headed by Senator Muskie or Senator Humphrey.

The 1972 Republican national convention had all the strengths and all the weaknesses of a Type B Convention. Except for a few voices such as those of Congressman Pete

McCloskey of California on the left and John Ashbrook of Ohio on the right, the convention was one of exquisite harmony. The high level of harmony, though, was accompanied by an equally high level of languor. As we mentioned in Chapter Three, the great strength of the Type B convention is the harmony that unites all factions of the party and allows the renominated incumbent to enter the campaign with the full backing of his party. On the other hand, the weakness of the Type B convention has historically been its lack of vitality, its inability to motivate the thousands of campaign workers who are frequently the essential ingredients of a political victory. The comparison between the Democratic primaries and the Republican primaries in the spring of 1972 is a real-life example of the phenomenon we are talking about. The Democratic primaries saw thousands and thousands of campaign workers intensely involved in efforts to win particular states for their chosen candidates. On the Republican side, at the same time, the campaign was one of listlessness bred of foreknowledge of who the victor would be and a concomitant lack of energy and enthusiasm.

The Republican campaign, like the Democratic campaign, began in New Hampshire in early February. The three principal actors in this primary were President Nixon, Congressman Paul N. (Pete) McCloskey from California, and John Ashbrook from Ohio. McCloskey was challenging President Nixon from the left and Ashbrook from the right. Ashbrook accused the President of departing from traditional Republican orthodoxy by turning to wage and price controls on the economic front and by moving away from Nationalist China and toward Mainland China and the Soviet Union on the international front. McCloskey faulted the president for his failure to end the war in Viet Nam and for his lack of enthusiasm in pushing for more progressive civil rights and civil liberties legislation. Neither congressman made a significant dent in the President's appeal. McCloskey received somewhat less than 21 percent of the vote in New Hampshire and thereafter withdrew from active campaigning. Ashbrook concentrated his campaigning in Florida but received only 12 percent of the vote there. Ashbrook was not able to win any delegates, and McCloskey won only one reluctant delegate from New Mexico. The one delegate who was forced to cast his vote for McCloskey insisted all along that he was for President Nixon, but because McCloskey received 10 percent of the vote in New Mexico, he was forced to vote for him. Once their campaigns had collapsed, both McCloskey and Ashbrook concentrated their attentions on the platform and on the delegate selection procedures to be used in 1976.

As is typical of a Type B convention, attempts to modify the President's platform were quickly shunted aside. McCloskey's efforts to be heard at the convention were stifled, and he found himself being sent to subcommittees to air his grievances. Neither the full platform committee nor the convention itself ever heard from Pete McCloskey.

The fight over the delegate selection procedures to be used in 1976 was more lively. The critical issue here was whether the more liberally inclined industrial, urbanized northern states would have a greater say in the selection of future presidential nominees. The liberals, expecting that Nixon would lose some of those northern industrial states, wanted delegate bonuses for electing Republican governors and senators. Conservatives, on the other hand, wanted the bonuses only at the presidential level, where they were relatively certain that their states would go Republican. In spite of some compromise, the plan worked out for the new delegate selection procedures is basically the one favored by conservatives.

Two of the most unusual features of the 1972 Republican national convention were the strident attacks made on the opposition and the presence of pro-Nixon Democrats such as the wife of the Democratic mayor of Milwaukee, Henry Maier, among the platform speakers. Frequently at Type B conventions the opposition is either ignored or treated rather gingerly. In 1964, the Democrats went to great lengths to make their convention as non-partisan as possible in order to attract Republicans to the Democratic nominee Lyndon Johnson. Apparently though, the Republicans in 1972 felt that George McGovern was so vulnerable that they could attract Democrats

to the Nixon camp by attacking the McGovern team and attempting to split Democratic regulars off from the new Mc-
Govern Democrats.

It was obvious that the Republicans had conducted a strong
Type B convention with the emphasis on harmony. The Republicans had made significant efforts to increase the vitality
and enthusiasm at their convention. Fears of apathy and its
effects were constantly aired by party leaders, who were making
obvious attempts to provoke the party activists into a more con-
certed campaign effort.

The Democrats, on the other hand, had destroyed both of the
major strengths of their Type A convention. With their new
delegate selection procedures, they did an effective job of lim-
iting or reducing the vitality and enthusiasm normally inherent
in a Type A convention by raising the possibility that the
party's nominee might not have won under the traditional rules.
And the Eagleton affair at the very beginning of the campaign
seriously disrupted the compromises that must be made to bring
harmony to a party that has only recently concluded a long
competition in the primaries.

One concluding note should be suggested about a fact of
contemporary life that is becoming increasingly important in
presidential campaigns. Before the introduction of radio, that
is, in the presidential elections from 1824 through 1916, the
average popular vote advantage for incumbents was only 2.5
percent. On the average, that is, incumbents received only 2.5
percent more votes than their opponents during this entire 92-
year period. As we moved into the age of radio, the years 1920
through 1948, the advantage to incumbents rose. During the age
of radio incumbents received on the average 8.91 percent more
votes than their opponents. Now we have now moved into the
age of television. During the period from 1952 to the present,
the average victory margin for incumbents has increased to
more than 19 percent.

If we look at presidential nominations during these three time
periods, we find that during the first period four presidents were
denied renomination. Since the radio age began, no president

has been denied renomination, which suggests that the mass media, and television in particular, have been astoundingly important in making the president not only a household word, but also a political figure of star proportions who is increasingly difficult to defeat.

CHAPTER SIXTEEN

Conclusion

The process of selecting a person to be the president of the United States is extraordinarily complicated. The candidate must not only battle his way through the primaries or through the nonprimary state conventions but also emerge victorious at his party's nominating convention before he takes on the leadership of the opposition party.

We have argued that the selection of the American president is strongly influenced by the cohesion and the vitality of the two major political parties. The strength and the cohesion of these parties, in turn, can frequently be discerned in the behavior of the two major political party nominating conventions normally held every fourth year. The depth of conflict that exists between the major factions of the two parties also becomes apparent at the conventions as do the vigor and enthusiasm with which party workers will attempt to maintain control over their own partisans and increase the party's percentage of the voters just entering the national political scene.

Our contention in this book has not been that the national party conventions cause electoral outcomes but rather that the national party conventions are indicators of the strength and cohesiveness the major parties possess as they move into the campaigns for the American presidency. We have suggested that under some conditions conflict is a valuable ingredient in a party's nominating convention. Conflict may indicate that a party has been successful in the preceding congressional elections and has ample candidates competing for the right to be the party's presidential nominee. The conflict that accompanies some types of elections also demonstrates vitality within the party because it signifies that there are strong candidates within the party who believe that the party's presidential nomination is worth fighting for.

Too much conflict, on the other hand, may indicate that the party is seriously divided, that one major faction of the party may refuse to back the party's presidential candidate, or that the high level of conflict within the party has sapped the party's strength and vitality, leaving it vulnerable to the opposition.

Harmony may, in some instances, be an indication that a party, especially a party that controls the present administration, has been able to overcome any major divisions that may have existed within its ranks and is basically unified on both the party platform and the presidential nominee.

Under different circumstances, harmony within the party convention may indicate that the party is lacking in vitality or that the party leaders do not feel the party's nomination is important enough for them to spend their energy and resources in attempting to acquire it. Harmonious conventions may also indicate the party's lack of electoral success in the last congressional and gubernatorial elections. Such a dearth of recent success at the polls may leave the party, as it did the Republican party in 1936, in a position where there are few presidential contenders. Under these conditions, harmony at the convention may indicate that the party's chances in the upcoming presidential election are almost nil.

While a harmonious convention can be an indicator that the party's chances are very good, so can one marked by conflict. Under certain circumstances conflict may indicate simply that a vital, aggressive, successful party is ironing out some of its difficulties and attempting to choose its ticket from among several contenders. Under other circumstances, conflict within the party means that the party is being torn apart, with large factions at such serious odds with other factions that there is little chance that the party can present a unified front for the November election. Conflict in an incumbent party may indicate that there is serious dissatisfaction with the performance of the party's president. It is difficult to convince the electorate that the party has successfully administered to the nation's needs during the previous four years, when the party itself is unconvinced that its presidential nominee is the best that it can offer.

In suggesting that the levels of harmony and conflict in national party conventions are important indicators of party strength and cohesion and, thus, of a party's chance for electoral victory in the presidential elections, we are not arguing that the conventions cause electoral success. Rather, we are arguing that the conventions are indicators of the probability that a party will be strong enough or cohesive enough or vigorous enough to defeat the opposition and, therefore, win the coveted prize of the American presidency.

Our argument is not intended to indicate that the national party conventions have not been changing. On the contrary, we notice that various convention types were more frequent during the 1800's than they are today, and we find that the roles played by media and public opinion polls are increasing in importance. Certainly the impact of the electronic media on the outcome of presidential elections cannot be denied. We are simply attempting to demonstrate that one indicator of electoral success is the nature of the presidential nominating conventions. The roles played by the media, by public opinion polls, and by other variables extraneous to our current study are considerations for another book at another time.

Notwithstanding the importance of the media and other public opinion-influencing devices, for the foreseeable future the conventions should continue to provide strong indications as to the condition of the two major parties and as to the probability that one party is in much better condition than the other to surmount the difficulties that face presidential candidates and to go on to win the office of the most powerful man on earth.

Bibliography

A GENERAL SURVEY OF PRESIDENTIAL ELECTIONS

Bean, Louis H. *How To Predict Elections.* New York: Knopf, 1948.

Cornell, Margaret. *The Machinery of the United States Presidential Election, A Summary of the Procedure.* Oxford: Oxford University Press, 1960.

Dulce, Berton, and Edward J. Richter. *Religion and the Presidency, A Recurring American Problem,* New York: Macmillan, 1962.

Jennings, M. Kent, and L. Harmon Zeigler. *The Electoral Process.* Englewood Cliffs, New Jersey: Prentice-Hall, 1966.

League of Women Voters of the United States. *Choosing the President.* Washington, D.C.: League of Women Voters of the United States, 1964.

League of Women Voters of the United States. *Who Should Elect the President?* Washington, D.C.: League of Women Voters of the United States, 1969.

Link, Arthur S. *Wilson. The Road to the White House.* Princeton, New Jersey: Princeton University Press, 1947.

Moos, Malcolm Charles. *Politics, Presidents, and Coattails.* Baltimore: Johns Hopkins, 1952.

Nebraska Debate Research Co. *Complete Handbook on Presidential Elections.* Lincoln: Nebraska Debate Research Co., 1953.

New York Times. *Elections—U.S.A., A Selection of Articles* from The New York Times Magazine. ed. by Evron M. Kirkpatrick and Jeane J. Kirkpatrick. New York: Rinehart and Winston, 1956.

Ogden, Daniel, and Arthur L. Peterson. *Electing the President.* Rev. ed. San Francisco: Chandler Publishing Co., 1968.

Paulsen, Pat. *How To Wage a Successful Campaign for the Presidency.* Los Angeles: Nash, 1972.

Pike, James. *A Roman Catholic in the White House.* Garden City, New York: Doubleday, 1960.

Peirce, Neal R. *The People's President*. New York: Simon & Schuster, 1968.

Pomper, Gerald Marvin. *Elections in America*. New York: Dodd, Mead, 1968.

Rogers, Will. *How We Elect Our President*. Selected and edited by Donald Day. Boston: Little, Brown & Co., 1952.

Sayre, Wallace S., and Judith H. Pappis. *Voting for President*. Washington, D.C.: Brookings Institution, 1970.

Scammon, Richard Montgomery, and Kenneth J. Wattinberg. *The Real Majority*. New York: Coward, McCann, 1970.

Schlesinger, Arthur M., Dr. (Ed.) *The Coming to Power: Critical Presidential Elections in American History*. New York: McGraw-Hill, 1972.

Schlesinger, Arthur, Jr. (Ed.) *History of American Presidential Elections, 1789–1968*. New York: Chelsea House, 1971. 4 vols.

Stanwood, Edward. *A History of Presidential Elections*. 3rd ed. Boston: Houghton Mifflin, 1892.

Warren, Sidney. *The Battle for the Presidency*. Philadelphia: Lippincott, 1968.

Weingast, David Elliott. *We Elect a President*. Rev. ed. New York: Messner, 1968.

PRESIDENTIAL ELECTIONS IN HISTORICAL CONTEXT

Chester, Lewis, Godfrey Hodgson, and Bruce Page, *An American Melodrama: The Presidential Campaign of 1968*. New York: Viking Press, 1969.

Clancy, Herbert John. *The Presidential Election of 1880*. Chicago: Loyola University Press, 1958.

Coleman, Charles Hubert. *The Election of 1868: The Democratic Efforts To Regain Control*. New York: Columbia University Press, 1933.

Cummings, Milton C. (Ed.) *The National Election of 1964*. Washington, D.C.: Brookings Institution, 1966.

Glad, Paul W. *McKinley, Bryan, and the People*. Philadelphia: Lippincott, 1964.

Guilfoyle, James H. *On the Trail of the Forgotten Man: A Journal of the Roosevelt Presidential Campaign*, Boston: Peabody Master Printers, 1933.

Jones, Stanley Llewellyn. *The Presidential Election of 1896*. Madison: University of Wisconsin Press, 1964.

Kelley, Frank K. *The Fight for the White House: The Story of 1912*. New York: Crowell, 1961.

Knoles, George Harmon. *The Presidential Campaign and Election of 1892.* Stanford: Stanford University Press, 1942.

Lamb, Karl A., and Paul A. Smith. *Campaign Decision-Making: The Presidential Election of 1964.* Belmont, Calif.: Wadsworth, 1968.

Lokos, Lionel. *Hysteria 1964: The Fear Campaign Against Barry Goldwater.* New Rochelle: Arlington House, 1967.

McGinniss, Joe. *The Selling of the President 1968.* New York: Trident Press, 1969.

Moore, Edmund Arthur. *A Catholic Runs for President: One Campaign of 1928.* New York: Ronald Press, 1956.

Morrison, S.E., "The First National Nominating Convention," *American Historical Review,* 17 (1912), 744–63.

Moscow, Warren. *Roosevelt and Willkie.* Englewood Cliffs, New Jersey: Prentice-Hall, 1968.

Norton, Lee. *War Elections, 1862–1864.* New York: International Publishers, 1944.

Parmet, Herbert S., and Marie B. Hecht. *Never Again: A President Runs for a Third Term.* New York: Macmillan, 1968.

Peel, Roy Victor, and Thomas C. Donnelly. *The 1932 Campaign: An Analysis.* New York: Farrar and Rinehart, 1935.

Peel, Roy Victor, and Thomas C. Donnelly. *The 1928 Campaign: An Analysis.* New York: R. R. Smith, 1931.

Roseboom, Eugene H. *A History of Presidential Elections.* New York: Macmillan, 1959.

Ross, Irwin. *The Loneliest Campaign, The Truman Victory of 1948,* New York: New American Library, 1968.

Thomas, Harrison Cook. *The Return of the Democratic Party to Power in 1884.* ("Studies in History, Economics, and Public Law." Vol. 89) New York: Columbia University, 1919.

Weeks, Oliver Douglas. *The Democratic Victory of 1932.* Dallas: Southern Methodist University, 1937.

Whicher, George F. (Ed.) *William Jennings Bryan and the Campaign of 1896.* Boston: D.C. Heath, 1953.

White, Theodore H. *The Making of the President 1960.* New York: Atheneum, 1961.

White, Theodore H. *The Making of the President 1964.* New York: Atheneum, 1965.

White, Theodore H. *The Making of the President 1968.* New York: Atheneum, 1969.

Wilensky, Norman M. *Conservatives in the Progressive Era: The Taft Republicans of 1942.* Gainesville: University of Florida Press, 1965.

Williams, Robert L. "The Presidential Election of 1904." Unpublished master's thesis, University of California, Berkeley, 1937.

PRESIDENTIAL CANDIDATES AND THEIR MEMOIRS

Barnard, Harry. *Rutherford B. Hayes and His America.* Indianapolis: Bobbs-Merrill, 1954.

Caldwell, Robert Granville. *James A. Garfield, Party Chieftain.* New York: Dodd, Mead, 1931.

Childs, Marquis. *Eisenhower: Captive Hero.* New York: Harcourt, Brace, and World, 1958.

Congressional Quarterly Service. *Historical Review of Presidential Candidates from 1788 to 1968; Including 3rd Parties, 1832–1968, With Popular and Electoral Vote.* 5th ed. Washington, D.C.: Congressional Quarterly Service, 1969.

Dunn, Arthur Wallace. *From Harrison to Harding.* New York: Putnam, 1922.

Eckenrode, H.J. *Rutherford B. Hayes, Statesman of Reform.* New York: Dodd, Mead, 1930.

Freidel, Frank. *Franklin D. Roosevelt, The Ordeal.* Boston: Little, Brown, 1954.

Freidel, Frank. *Franklin D. Roosevelt, The Triumph.* Boston: Little, Brown, 1956.

Gosnell, Harold F. *Champion Campaigner, Franklin D. Roosevelt.* New York: Macmillan, 1952.

Hesseltine, William G. *Ulysses S. Grant, Politician.* New York: Dodd, Mead, 1935.

Hoover, Herbert C. *Memoirs, The Cabinet and the Presidency, 1920–1933.* New York: Macmillan, 1952.

Howe, George Frederick. *Chester A. Arthur, A Quarter-Century of Machine Politics.* New York: Dodd, Mead, 1934.

Judah, Charles Burnett, and George Winston Smith. *The Unchosen.* New York: Coward, McCann, 1962.

McElroy, Robert. *Grover Cleveland, The Man and the Statesman.* New York: Harper and Bros., 1923.

Nevins, Allan. *Grover Cleveland: A Study in Courage.* New York: Dodd, Mead, 1932.

Northrop, Henry Davenport. *The Life and Public Services of Benjamin Harrison, The Great American Statesman.* Philadelphia: National Publishing Co., 1891.

Pringle, Henry F. *The Life and Times of William Howard Taft.* New York: Farrar and Rinehart, 1939, Vol. 2.

Robinson, Lloyd. *The Hopefuls: Ten Presidential Campaigns.* New York: Doubleday, 1966.

Seitz, Don Carlos. *The "Also Rans": Great Men Who Missed Making the Presidential Goal.* Freeport: Books for Libraries Press, 1968.

Sisners, Harry J., S.J. *Benjamin Harrison, Hoosier Statesman.* New York: University Publications, 1959.

Smith, Theodore Clarke. *The Life and Letters of James Abram Garfield.* New Haven, Connecticut: Yale University Press, 1925.

Truman, Harry S. *Memoirs.* New York: Doubleday, 1956.

Young, Kylde, and Lamar Middleton. *Heirs-Apparent: The Vice-Presidents of the United States.* New York: Prentice-Hall, 1948.

THE FINANCING OF PRESIDENTIAL ELECTIONS
AND GENERAL DOCUMENTS AND STATISTICS

Alexander, Herbert E. *Financing the 1960 Election.* Princeton, New Jersey: Citizen's Research Foundation, 1964.

Alexander, Herbert E. *Financing the 1964 Election.* Princeton, New Jersey: Citizen's Research Foundation, 1966.

Alexander, Herbert E. (Ed.) *Money for Politics: A Miscellany of Ideas.* Princeton, New Jersey: Citizens Research Foundation, 1963.

Bibby, John F. *The Politics of National Convention Finances and Arrangements.* Princeton, New Jersey: Citizen's Research Foundation, 1968.

Burnham, Walter D. *Presidential Ballots, 1836–1892.* Baltimore: Johns Hopkins Press, 1955.

Dunn, Delmer D. *Financing Presidential Campaigns.* Washington, D.C.: Brookings Institution, 1972.

Governmental Affairs Institute, Selections Research Center. *America at the Polls: A Handbook of American Presidential Selection Statistics, 1920–1964.* Ed. by Richard M. Scammon. Pittsburgh: University of Pittsburgh Press, 1965.

Hennessy, Bernard. *Dollars for Democrats, 1959.* New Brunswick, New Jersey: Eagleton Institute, 1960.

McKee, Thomas H. *The National Conventions and Platforms of All Political Parties.* 6th ed. Baltimore: Truedenward, 1906.

Overacker, Louise. *Presidential Campaign Funds.* Gaspar C. Bacon Lectureship on the Constitution of the United States. ("Boston University Lectures, 1945.") Boston: Boston University Press, 1946.

Petersen, Svend. *A Statistical History of the American Presidential Elections.* New York: Ungar, 1963.

Porter, Kirk H., and Donald B. Johnson. *National Party Platforms 1840–1956.* Urbana: University of Illinois Press, 1956.

President's Commission on Campaign Costs. *Financing Presidential Campaigns, Report of the President's Commission on Campaign Costs.* Washington, D.C.: Government Printing Office, 1962.

Robinson, Edgar Eugene. *The Presidential Vote, 1896–1932.* Palo Alto: Stanford University Press, 1934.

Robinson, Edgar Eugene. *They Voted for Roosevelt: The Presidential Vote, 1932–1944.* Palo Alto: Stanford University Press, 1947.

Runyon, John J., et al. *Source Book on American Presidential Campaign and Election Statistics, 1948–68.* Compiled and edited by

John H. Runyon, Jennifer Verdini, and Sally S. Runyon. New York: Ungar, 1971.

Scammon, Richard M. (ed.) *America at the Polls: A Handbook of American Presidential Election Statistics, 1920–64*. Compiled and edited for Governmental Affairs Institute. Pittsburgh: University of Pittsburgh Press, 1965.

Stoddard, Henry. *It Costs To Be President*. New York: Harper and Bros., 1938.

Twentieth Century Fund. *Voters' Time: Report of The Twentieth Century Fund Commission on Campaign Costs in the Electronic Era*. New York: Twentieth Century Fund, 1969.

U.S. Senate. *Nomination and Selection of the President and Vice President of the United States Including the Manner of Selecting Delegates to National Political Conventions*. Washington, D.C.: Government Printing Office, 1964.

U.S. Library of Congress. *Select List of References on Corrupt Practices in Elections*. Compiled under Direction of Appleton, Prentice & Clark, Friggin. Washington, D.C.: Government Printing Office, 1908.

U.S. Senate. Special Committee Investigating Presidential Campaign Expenditure: *Presidential Campaign Expenditures*. Washington, D.C.: Government Printing Office, 1928.

THE STRATEGY AND TACTICS OF
PRESIDENTIAL ELECTIONS

Baus, Herbert M., and William B. Ross. *Politics Battle Plan*. New York: Macmillan, 1968.

Bean, Louis Hyman. *Ballot Behavior: A Study of Presidential Elections*. Washington, D.C.: American Council on Public Affairs, 1940.

Bean, Louis Hyman. *How America Votes in Presidential Elections*. Metuchen, N.J.: Scarecrow Press, 1968.

Brown, William Burlie. *The People's Choice: The Presidential Image in the Campaign Biography*. Baton Rouge: Louisiana State University Press, 1960.

Bruno, Jerry, and Jeff Greenfield. *The Advance Man*. New York: Morrow, 1971.

Campbell, Angus, P. Converse, W. Miller, and D. Stokes. *The American Voter*. New York: Wiley, 1960.

Campbell, Angus, and Robert L. Kahn. *The People Elect a President*. Ann Arbor: Survey Research Center, Institute for Social Research, University of Michigan, 1952.

Campbell, Angus, G. Gurin, and W. Miller. *The Voter Decides*. Evanston, Ill.: Row, Peterson, 1954.

Democratic National Committee. *Victory '68*. Democratic Campaign

Handbook of 1968. Washington, D.C.: Democratic National Committee, 1968.

Flanigan, William H. *Political Behavior of the American Electorate.* Boston: Allyn & Bacon, 1968.

Gosnell, Harold Foote. *Grass Roots Politics: National Voting Behavior of Typical States.* Washington, D.C.: American Council on Public Affairs, 1942.

Kelley, Stanley. *Professional Public Relations and Political Power.* Baltimore: Johns Hopkins Press, 1956.

Kessel, John Howard. *The Goldwater Coalition: Republican Strategies in 1964.* Indianapolis: Bobbs-Merrill, 1968.

Key, V.O., Jr. *The Responsible Electorate, Rationality in Presidential Voting, 1936—1960.* Cambridge: Belknap Press, 1966.

Kingdon, John W. *Candidates for Office, Beliefs and Strategies.* New York: Random House, 1968.

Moon, Henry Lee. *Balance of Power: The Negro Vote.* Garden City, N.Y.: Doubleday, 1949.

Napolitan, Joseph. *The Election Game and How To Win It.* Garden City, N.Y.: Doubleday, 1972.

Polsby, Nelson W., and Aaron B. Wildavsky. *Presidential Elections, Strategies of American Electoral Politics.* 2nd ed. New York: Scribner's, 1968.

Shadegg, Stephen C. *How To Win an Election: The Art of Political Victory.* New York: Taplinger, 1964.

Thomson, Charles A. *Television and Presidential Politics: The Experience of 1952 and the Problems Ahead.* Washington, D.C.: Brookings Institution, 1956.

Wallace, David. *First Tuesday: A Study of Rationality in Voting.* Garden City, N.Y.: Doubleday, 1964.

Weisbord, Marvin Ross. *Campaigning for President: A New Look at the Road to the White House.* Washington, D.C.: Public Affairs Press, 1964.

Wycoff, Gene. *The Image Candidates: American Politics in the Age of Television.* New York: Macmillan, 1968.

CANDIDATE SELECTION PRIMARIES, CONVENTIONS, AND THE ELECTORAL COLLEGE

American Bar Association. *Electing the President.* A Report of The Commission on Electoral College Reform. Chicago: American Bar Association, 1967.

American Enterprise Institute for Public Policy Research. *Proposals for Revision of the Electoral College System.* Washington, D.C.: The Institute, 1969.

American Political Science Association. Committee on Political Parties. *Toward a More Responsible Two-Party System.* New York: Rinehart, 1950.

Bailey, Stephen K. *The Condition of Our National Political Parties.* New York: Fund for the Republic, 1959.

Bain, Richard C. *Convention Decisions and Voting Records.* Washington, D.C.: Brookings Institution, 1960.

Beman, L.T. (ed.) *Abolishment of the Electoral College.* New York: H.W. Wilson, 1926.

Bendiner, Robert. *White House Fever: An Innocent's Guide to Principles and Practices, Respectable and Otherwise, Behind the Election of American Presidents.* New York: Harcourt, Brace, 1960.

Bickel, Alexander M. *Reform and Continuity: The Electoral College, The Convention, and The Party System.* New York: Harper & Row, 1971.

Bishop, Joseph Bucklin. *Presidential Nominations and Elections: A History of American Conventions, National Campaigns, Inaugurations and Campaign Caricature.* New York: Scribner's, 1916.

Bone, Hugh A. *Party Committees and National Politics.* Seattle: University of Washington Press, 1958.

Brooks, Robert. *Political Parties and Electoral Problems.* 3rd ed. New York: Harper & Bros., 1933.

Columbia University Teachers College, Citizenship Education Project. *Political Parties and Presidential Elections.* New York: Columbia University, 1970.

Commission on Party Structure and Delegate Selection. *Mandate for Reform.* Report of Commission on Party Structure and Delegate Selection to the Democratic National Committee. Washington, D.C.: Democratic National Committee, 1970.

Congressional Quarterly Service. *The Presidential Nominating Conventions, 1968.* Washington, D.C.: Congressional Quarterly Service, 1968.

Daniels, Walter Machray (ed.). *Presidential Election Reforms.* New York: H.W. Wilson, 1953.

David, Paul T., and Ralph M. Goldman, and Richard C. Bain. *The Politics of National Party Conventions.* Washington, D.C.: Brookings Institution, 1960.

David, Paul Theodore, Malcolm Moos, and Ralph M. Goldman. *Presidential Nominating Politics in 1952.* 5 Vols. Baltimore: Johns Hopkins Press, 1954.

David, Paul. *The Role of Governors at the National Party Conventions.* Washington, D.C. Brookings Institution, 1960.

Davis, James W. *Presidential Primaries: Road to the White House.* New York: Crowell, 1967.

Dougherty, John Hampden. *The Electoral System of the United States: Its History, Together with a Study of the Perils That Have Attended Its Operations.* New York: Putnam, 1906.

Eaton, Herbert. *Presidential Timber: A History of Nominating Conventions, 1868–1960.* New York: Free Press of Glencoe, 1964.

Farley, James A. *Behind the Ballots.* New York: Harcourt, Brace, 1938.

Flynn, Edward J. *You're the Boss.* New York: Viking, 1947.

Fuller, Robert Higginson. *Government by the People: The Laws & Customs Regulating the Electoral System & The Formation & Control of Political Parties in the United States.* New York: Macmillan, 1908.

Goss, Hilton P. "The Pre-Convention Presidential Campaign of 1912." Unpublished Ph.D. dissertation, University of California, Berkeley, 1942.

Harris, Joseph Pratt. *Election Administration in the United States.* Washington, D.C.: Brookings Institution, 1934.

Johnsen, J.E. (ed.). *Direct Election of the President.* New York: H.W. Wilson, 1949.

Johnson, Walter, *How We Drafted Adlai Stevenson.* New York: Knopf, 1955.

Josephson, Matthew. *The President Makers: The Culture of Politics and Leadership in an Age of Enlightenment, 1896–1919.* New York: Harcourt, Brace, 1940.

Kefauver, Estes. "Indictment of the Political Convention." *New York Times Magazine,* March 16, 1952.

Longley, Lawrence D., and Alan G. Braun. *The Politics of Electoral College Reform.* New Haven, Conn.: Yale University Press, 1972.

MacBride, Roger Lea. *The American Electoral College.* Caldwell, Idaho: Caxton Printers, 1953.

Martin, Ralph G. *The Bosses.* New York: Putnam, 1964.

McClure, A.K. *Our Presidents and How We Make Them.* New York: Harper & Bros. 1902.

Mencken. H.L. *Making a President.* New York: Knopf, 1932.

Menman, Charles Edward, and Louise Overacker. *Primary Elections.* Chicago: University of Chicago Press, 1928.

Michener, James A. *Presidential Lottery: The Reckless Gamble in Our Electoral System.* New York: Random House, 1969.

Ostrogorskii, M. "The Rise And Fall of the Nominating Caucus, Legislative and Congressional." *American Historical Review,* 5(January 1900), 255–59.

Overacker, Louise. *The Presidential Primary.* New York: Macmillan, 1926.

Pappis, Judith H. *The Convention Problem: Issues in Reform of*

Presidential Nominative Procedures. Washington, D.C.: Brookings Institution, 1972.

Polsby, Nelson. "Decision-Making at the National Conventions," *Western Political Quarterly,* 13(September 1960).

Pomper, Gerald. *Nominating the President.* Evanston, Ill.: Northwestern University Press, 1963.

Prufer, Julius Fielding. *American Political Parties and Presidential Elections.* Philadelphia: McKinley Publishing, 1932.

State University of Iowa, Institute of Public Affairs. *A Report on Presidential Primary Laws.* Iowa City: State University of Iowa Press, 1953.

Stoddard, Henry Luther. *Presidential Sweepstakes, The Story of Political Conventions and Campaigns.* Ed. by Frances W. Leary. New York: G. P. Putnam's Sons, 1948.

Stone, Kathryn H. (Meyers). *Choosing the President of the U.S.A.* New York: Carrie Chapman Catt Memorial Fund, 1955.

Thompson, Charles S. *The Rise and Fall of the Congressional Caucus.* New Haven, Conn.: Yale University Press, 1902.

Tillett, Paul (ed.) *Inside Politics: The National Conventions, 1960.* Dobbs Ferry, N.Y.: Oceana Publications, 1962.

Tugwell, R.G. *How They Became President: Thirty-Five Ways to the White House.* New York: Simon & Schuster, 1964.

Wilmending, Lucius. *The Electoral College.* New Brunswick, N.J.: Rutgers University Press, 1958.

Index